Welcome...

Welcome to my guide to the wines of Bordeaux. It is a guide that reflects my love for the wines of this fantastic region in all forms; the dry white, red and seductively sweet Sauternes. It should be of interest to everyone, from the most knowledgeable drinker of Bordeaux, to the aspirational newcomer...and all in between. I hope it may even instil in you some sense of the passion I feel for this fascinating region of France, but before we get to that, perhaps I should tell you a little about myself.

My Story

To understand where my passion comes from, let me take you back in time a couple of decades. My early experiences of Bordeaux were not with the very grandest of wines. Good wines, yes, but not the iconic names that easily impress. One of the very first I encountered was the 1985 vintage, from Château Rauzan-Ségla in the Margaux appellation. This château had been highly ranked in the past but, like many estates in Bordeaux, the ravages of phylloxera and mildew (devastating vine diseases newly imported from North America during the late 19th century), followed by world war and global economic depression, had taken their toll.

Nevertheless, despite a less than glowing reputation, the 1985 Rauzan-Ségla, poured for me by a generous host, was pretty good. The key here was my friend's inside knowledge; he was aware that new proprietors were investing in the property and vineyards in a bid to turn around both the quality of wine and the château's fortunes. Armed with this knowledge he got in early and acquired (what would become) a top wine at a favourable price. This is one key to getting the best from Bordeaux; know which of the châteaux are on the up, and you'll know where your cash is best spent.

Fast forward a few years and a different, but equally generous, host poured for me a glass of the 1990 vintage from Château Barreyres, a small estate very near the Gironde, tucked away between the two very famous communes of St Julien to the north and Margaux to the south. This was uncommonly good, I thought, and I can still taste its slightly minty blackcurrant fruit and sense the texture on my palate today, more than twenty years later. Here were more valuable lessons to be learnt concerning Bordeaux; don't forget to look beyond the big names for your wines, know those estates that are excluded from grand classifications and yet turn out excellent wines, and make sure you snap them up when a truly great vintage – such as 1990 – comes along.

The common theme here is that my two hosts clearly knew Bordeaux very well. My own response to this might perhaps come as no surprise. Before long I was tasting and drinking everything from the cheap-and-cheerful, through to the finest premier grand cru classé. I devoured every piece of information on Bordeaux I could find, and after a decade felt I knew the subject well enough to begin writing, instead of only reading, about wine.

It was in May 2000 that I launched my website, Winedoctor (www.thewinedoctor.com). Although my remit was broad (I have featured wines from the world over on Winedoctor) I have always demonstrated a leaning towards Bordeaux (and, I should also mention, the wines of the Loire Valley). Indeed, two of the very first reports I posted on Winedoctor concerned tastings of the 1988 and 1989 Bordeaux vintages. Over the years Winedoctor has grown into a huge resource, but has never turned it's back on Bordeaux. I travel to the region regularly, including trips there to taste during the all-important primeurs week, when the latest vintage is shown to the world's wine press, and my reports are published on Winedoctor.

So it's safe to say that those early bottles of Rauzan-Ségla and Barreyres fired my enthusiasm for Bordeaux as a region. But what about you, the 21st century reader? Clearly developing an intricate knowledge of the region and wines through visiting – as I myself have done – isn't the answer for everybody. My website can give you all the information you need, with a detailed, meticulous approach. But we are all over-worked and short on time, so I decided that a portable MagBook of abridged profiles and digestible guidance, to include advice on purchasing, cellaring, decanting, investing, drinking and even enjoying Bordeaux, in both print and electronic formats, would be worthwhile.

Who Should Read This Guide

Bordeaux is ever-changing, and yet some things remain immutable. This guide deals with both extremes and everything inbetween, making it broadly useful to all. I cover the latest news from the region in chapter 2, which should serve the needs of initiated drinkers of Bordeaux, while for those less familiar with the wines my guide to the region, with detailed accounts of the communes, wines and classifications in chapter 10, as well as my guide to enjoying Bordeaux in chapter 11, may be most useful. For those that lie between these two, my profiles of the best and best-value châteaux in chapters 5 and 7 should prove of interest, as should my Money Matters reports in chapter 12.

Annual Guides: The Problems and The Solutions

One of the problems inherent in print publishing, as opposed to an instantaneous medium such as the internet, is that print guides are always going to be dated. Take your typical annual pocket wine guide; in order for it to be on the shelves before Christmas the finished manuscript has to be at the printers by September. That means the copy from all the different contributors has to be submitted for checking and proof-reading months before that. It is inevitable by the time you open the guide to read the 'latest' news, it will be nearly a year out of date. This guide is different. With as short an interval between writing and publication as possible, everything within these pages is up to date, checked and verified only a few weeks before publication.

Secondly, everything within this guide is written by me. This might seem obvious, but many annual pocket guides from famous names are in fact ghost-written by a team of contributors. This seems to me a system which can be improved upon, and so I give you this guarantee: every opinion expressed in this book, every profile of every château, every word of every section in this guide is my own. Where you would like more detail on a certain topic (bear in mind this is a pocket guide), and indeed for more on all of the subjects presented in this MagBook, do visit my website Winedoctor (www.thewinedoctor. com), which is updated on a daily basis.

With that, let me leave you with my one wish; regardless of your experience of Bordeaux, I hope this guide is of use to you, and that your drinking is enhanced by its presence on your bookshelf. After all, that is what it's all about!

EDITORIAL
Writer Chris Kissack
Contributor Tommy Melville
Art Editor Anand Parmar
Digital Production Manager
Nicky Baker

MANAGEMENT
MagBook Publisher Dharmesh Mistry
Production Director Robin Ryan
MD of Advertising Julian Lloyd-Evans
Newstrade Director David Barker
Commercial & Retail Director
Martin Belson
Chief Financial Officer Brett Reynolds
Group Finance Director Ian Leggett
Chief Executive James Tye
Chairman Felix Dennis

MAG**BOOK**

The MagBook brand is a trademark of
Dennis Publishing Ltd., 30 Cleveland St,
London W1T 4JD. Company registered in
England. All material © Dennis Publishing Ltd,
licensed by Felden 2012, and may not be
reproduced in whole or part without the
consent of the publishers.
Pocket Guide to the Wines of Bordeaux
ISBN 1-78106-065-7

LICENSING
To license this product, please contact
Carlotta Seratoni on +44 (0) 20 7907
6550, or email carlotta_serantoni@dennis.
co.uk. To syndicate content from this product
please contact Anj Dosaj Halai on +44(0)
20 7907 6132 or email anj_dosaj-halai@
dennis.co.uk

LIABILITY
While every care was taken during the
production of this MagBook, the publishers
cannot be held responsible for the accuracy
of the information or any consequence
arising from it. The paper used within this
MagBook is produced from sustainable fibre,
manufactured by mills with a valid chain of
custody. Printed at Stones.

Contents

Map of
Bordeaux Châteaux

Chapter 4
The Firsts

1. Château Latour
2. Château Lafite-Rothschild
3. Château Mouton-Rothschild
4. Château Margaux
5. Château Haut-Brion
6. Château d'Yquem
7. Château Cheval-Blanc
8. Château Ausone
9. Petrus
10. Le Pin

Chapter 5
Top 20 Châteaux

11. Château Pontet-Canet
12. Château Lynch-Bages
13. Château Léoville-Barton
14. Château Pichon-Lalande
15. Château Pichon-Baron
16. Château Léoville-Las-Cases
17. Château Montrose
18. Château Léoville-Poyferré
19. Château Ducru-Beaucaillou
20. Château Cos d'Estournel
21. Château Trotanoy
22. Château Grand-Puy-Lacoste
23. Château Calon-Ségur
24. Château Palmer
25. Château Smith-Haut-Lafitte
26. Domaine de Chevalier
27. Château Angélus
28. Vieux Château Certan
29. Château Haut-Bailly
30. Château Église-Clinet

Chapter 6
Top 5 Sauternes

31. Château Climens
32. Château Coutet
33. Château Rieussec
34. Château Suduiraut
35. Château Lafaurie-Peyraguey

Chapter 7
Top 10 Value

36. Château Sociando-Mallet
37. Château Cantemerle
38. Château Gloria
39. Château Brown
40. Château Chasse-Spleen
41. Château Angludet
42. Château Grand Mayne
43. Château Ormes de Pez
44. Château Raymond-Lafon
45. Château Doisy-Védrines

Chapter 8
Top 10 To Try

46. Château Brane-Cantenac
47. Château Gruaud-Larose
48. Château Lafon-Rochet
49. Château La Conseillante
50. Château Labégorce
51. Château Petit Village
52. Château La Pointe
53. Château Fourcas Hosten
54. Château La Vieille Cure
55. Château Hosanna

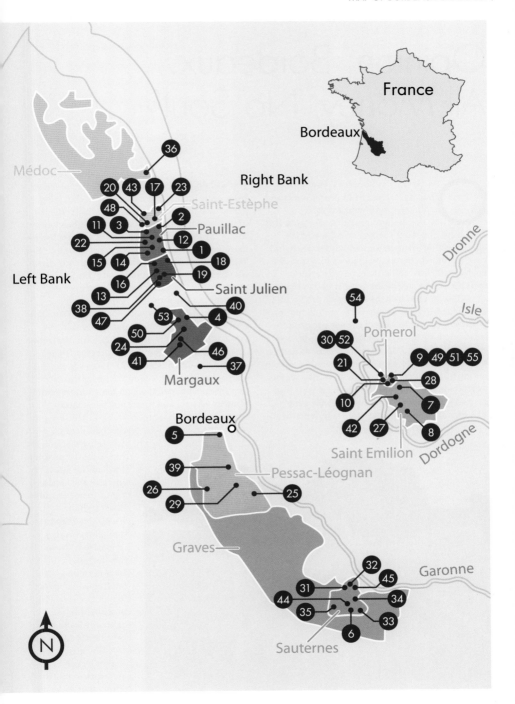

France

Bordeaux

Médoc

Right Bank

Left Bank

36

20 43 17 23

Saint-Estèphe

48

11 3 2

Pauillac

22

12

15 14 1

16 18

13 19

38 Saint Julien

47 40

53 4

50

24 46

41 37

Margaux

Dronne

Isle

54

30 52 Pomerol

21 9 49 51 55

28

10 7

42 27 8

Saint Emilion

Dordogne

Bordeaux

5

39

Pessac-Léognan

26

29 25

Graves

Garonne

32

45

31

44 34

35 33

6

Sauternes

N

Opinion: Bordeaux... All Money, No Soul?

On arriving at Bordeaux, you'll have hardly stepped from your aircraft and collected your luggage before bumping into your first vineyard. It is not a huge plot, admittedly, just a few rows of vines running between the arrivals terminal and parking lot, where row after row of hire cars line up. Nevertheless, could there be a stronger message of how significant wine is to this region?

Strike out towards the vineyards proper and what you encounter should serve only to reinforce Bordeaux's status as king of the wine regions. Head north through the Médoc communes and you will pass grand châteaux with famous names, each surrounded by expansive vineyards on gently rolling hills. But to really get to know this region, to get under its skin, you need to leave your hire car and walk among the vines, meet the people who own them, and talk to those who tend them.

You will find yourself receiving a warm welcome from some intensely knowledgeable, charming, passionate and opinionated individuals. They understand the soil, and they love it. They know where the finest grapes are grown, and use their many years of knowledge and experience to create the best wines possible. Their driving enthusiasm is to be envied and admired, and it is one of the many reasons that Bordeaux is enjoying such great success once again.

Come away from the region, though, and the view of Bordeaux from the outside couldn't be more different. Some of its critics have described it as soulless. In their eyes it is a region where accountants and business suits reign supreme, where the sale of wine (and thus its price) is heavily manipulated through the antiquated en primeur system, and where any one château represents little more than a brand name for a wine made from a disparate collection of vineyards, the product of which can't possibly represent the locality's origins in a true and honest fashion.

All too often these complaints involve comparisons drawn with Burgundy, Bordeaux's long-standing and always competitive rival. To cut straight to the chase, Bordeaux will never satisfy those who crave the intricacies brought by the patchwork of miniscule terroirs that make up

Burgundy. If you are allergic to marketing speak, and want to buy your wine from a vigneron with vineyard dirt beneath his fingernails, then perhaps Burgundy is a better option for you. And believe it or not, I have a lot of sympathy with these opinions. There's no denying that Bordeaux is big business these days, and its big business backers and bravado mean it certainly isn't for everybody.

But let's not forget those individuals I introduced you to only a few paragraphs ago. At ground level, Bordeaux is just as much about commitment and passion as Burgundy. The vineyards may be ten times larger (more, in some cases), and the proprietors may not take a hand in the everyday running of the estates, but let us not mistake that for disinterest or emotional detachment. These people – the Cathiards of Château Smith-Haut-Lafitte, the Vaulthiers of Château Ausone, the Borie family at Château Grand-Puy-Lacoste and Château Ducru-Beaucaillou – have Bordeaux flowing in their arteries, capillaries and veins. They and Bordeaux are one and the same. Half an hour in their company will soon put to bed any concerns that Bordeaux has no soul, or that disinterested proprietors consider their châteaux merely as a kind of cash cow.

This then begs the question; why is there such a strong undercurrent of anti-Bordeaux sentiment in the world of wine today? Why is it seen as soulless and uninspiring? There are many possible facets to this debate, but I think first and foremost is money. Bordeaux is very expensive, much more so than it has ever been, and it is only natural that

these price rises have influenced the way many drinkers view the region.

Just how much has Bordeaux risen in price? Back in 2002 I ran a quick rough-and-ready analysis of increases in wine prices against UK inflation, the UK not only being where I live but also a hub for much of the international wine trade. Comparing prices then with those from the 1980s, inflation had put up the cost of living by 76%, but over the same time period the price of top Bordeaux had risen by more than 500%. Repeating the exercise in early 2012, the cost of living in the UK is now 139% higher than it was during the 1980s, but many of Bordeaux's wines, bolstered by super-high prices in the 2009 and 2010 vintages, are now more than 2000% more expensive than they were thirty years ago. I provide more analysis of Bordeaux price rises, based on the Liv-ex indices, in chapter 12.

There are many different reasons why Bordeaux has seen such stratospheric rises in pricing. To some extent it reflects improved quality, and to some extent market demand; after all, the Bordalais would be fools to charge less than buyers are willing to pay. But there are other factors more recently arrived on the scene, including a more increased awareness of Bordeaux as a vehicle for investment, and also the opening up of markets where consumers are prepared to pay top prices for the very best (or, at least, what they perceive to be the best). This is particularly the case in the Asian markets, many of which are served by the tax-free environment enjoyed by Hong Kong-based traders.

Speculative rises in pricing inevitably lead to

the question of whether or not the international market for Bordeaux will crash. Such a dramatic development would not be without precedent; take a look back at the lists of London wine merchants published one hundred years ago and you will see the most expensive wines were not those from Bordeaux, but from Germany. But times, tastes and fashions have changed, and today Germany's superb Rieslings are globally under-appreciated and thus hugely under-valued. Will history repeat itself? Will the Bordeaux of 2050 be the cheapest option on the wine list, usurped by styles from other regions?

I would suggest not; it is only natural to dream of a future where we will be able to stock our cellars with the very best of Bordeaux, but I fear it unlikely. Although many hip sommeliers – an increasingly important driving force in determining wine trends – have turned their backs on Bordeaux, filling their list with more exciting, less familiar options, there are still too many interested consumers hankering after Bordeaux for prices to hit rock-bottom. Sure, we may see corrections like that at the end of 2011 when the year-on-year price fell by almost 15%, but the overall long-term trend is upwards, and a return to the pricing of ten or twenty years ago seems improbable. Secondly, the quality of modern Bordeaux is very high, somewhat justifying these higher prices, while in contrast Germany's price decline went hand in hand with falling quality. Thirdly, there is a great amount of wealth in the world; there are more millionaires and billionaires than ever, and many are

wine-interested, as an investment if not for drinking. Fourthly, new markets are opening up; China, India and Brazil are increasingly prosperous, and many of their wealthy inhabitants are thirsty!

None of this bodes well for the layman in the street, for those of us who drink to a budget. But fear not; there will always be value to be sniffed out in Bordeaux, of that we can be sure. There are many minor châteaux turning out affordable wines which age incredibly well, and undisputedly give that Bordeaux kick at palatable prices. This guide should help you discover them; and getting to know these wines, sometimes from small domaines and grimy-handed vignerons, rather than the wallet-busting first growths, will prove beyond doubt that Bordeaux has a soul. However, if my predictions are wrong, and prices crash down to match those of the 1980s, then at least you and I are prepared; simply turn to chapter four for guidance on whether you should head for Latour, Ausone, Margaux or Lafite-Rothschild.

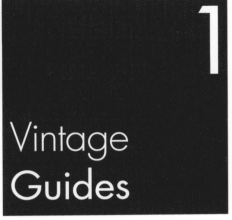

Vintage Guides

Knowledge of the latest vintages (and their respective qualities) remains essential. This chapter gives background information and buying recommendations tailored around recent vintages. In all cases I look for wines that might actually be affordable; after all, it is pointless drawing up a list populated by unaffordable first growths, and the like. Even in the most recent, highly priced vintages, I make sure to make some budget recommendations.

Introduction

The following pages give brief reports on the vintages from 2010 to 2003 (including a quick look at the 2002 – 1990 vintages). In each case I give some recommendations, but have avoided the very best wines of the vintage on grounds of exceedingly high price. It is easy to draw up a list of the very top wines – which would undoubtedly feature the likes of Ausone, Margaux, Latour and Petrus – based on reputation alone. Therefore I have focused on more affordable wines – wines for realists, as I have called them.

My cut-off is arbitrary, but for the left bank wines I have tried to focus on those in the lower half of the Liv-Ex 2011 classification (see page 132) where prices are likely to be more favourable. As for the right bank and Sauternes, or my 'value picks' in more recent vintages, I have opted for wines where the price seems to suit the quality, without breaking the bank. A word of warning though – these days 'value' Bordeaux remains expensive when viewed against the wider world of wine. Sadly, there are no 'cheap' wines here.

A BRIEF LOOK AT THE 2002 – 1990 VINTAGES

2002
A cooler year which produced good white wines and classically styled red wines. Always a vintage for buying the best.

2001
A very good year, but one regularly overshadowed by 2000. The Pomerols were top of the reds and the Sauternes were magnificent.

2000
Wonderful weather through August and September made fabulous red wines from both banks, the whites and Sauternes are less appealing.

1999
A wet and challenging vintage. Quality among the red wines is variable. The Sauternes are under-rated.

1998
A hot summer but a wet harvest, and it was a vintage where the Merlot-dominated right bank shone.

1997
An unexciting vintage for reds. The Sauternes are rich and enticing, though.

1996
Later picked Cabernets which escaped the rain on the left bank did best. Other regions fared less well.

1995
An all-round vintage blessed by an Indian summer. There are good wines from both banks. The Sauternes were good.

1994
Heavy September rains put a damper on things here. A

good, if rather leaner, style of red wine though.

1993
The last of three vintages dogged by rain, particularly in September. Good wines are few and far between – treat with caution.

1992
Heavy rain, in June, put paid to this vintage. Another to avoid.

1991
The first in a run of three dreadful vintages for Bordeaux.

1990
A great vintage, one of the best of the 20th century, to be grouped together with 1982, 1961 and 1945. Superlative wines of all colours, drinking well now.

Bordeaux 2010

This vintage was marked by a summer drought, but without the extremes of temperature suffered in other dry years, such as 2003. This tended to produce grapes with thick skins, rich in colour and tannin but fresh of flavour, rather than baked or raisined. There were also cool nights and a cooler August, both features working to preserve the acidity in the wines to match the substance and tannin that came from the skins. The most quality-orientated estates waited and waited for physiological ripeness; in some cases the traditional 100-day rule between flowering and harvest was more than 20% inaccurate.

Early tastings revealed the wines (or rather barrel samples) to be structured, less voluptuous than 2009, but rich in silky-sweet tannin and acidity. Success is rarely universal though, and the risk of drought means many of the greatest left bank cuvées are Cabernet-rich, often showing a greater dependence on Cabernet Sauvignon because this later-ripening variety fairs better than the earlier-ripening Merlot which has, in some plots, ended up very tannic and alcoholic. Strict selection meant these grapes were naturally excluded from the grands vins of the best estates. And on the right bank there was also evidence of

WINES TO BUY

In a great vintage such as 2010, the top châteaux should make brilliant wines. In recent years, however, the prices of these wines have carried them beyond the reach of most.

A Top Five for Realists
- Grand-Puy-Lacoste
- Malescot St-Exupéry
- Lafon-Rochet
- d'Issan
- Rauzan-Ségla

Bordeaux on a Budget
- Gloria
- La Goulée
- Tronquoy-Lalande
- Feytit-Clinet
- Les Ormes de Pez

drought difficulty, primarily with Merlot but not exclusively so; in some vineyards it was the Cabernet Franc that failed to cope with the shortage of water.

2010 produced many great wines; but in some respects we should consider these wines to have been created despite the climatic conditions of that year, rather than because of them (as was the case in 2009). That such success exists reflects the hard work undertaken in the cellars of Bordeaux, rather than the benevolence of Mother Nature. What we have is a vintage in which left bank Cabernet Sauvignon reigns supreme, although there are still some superb wines from the Merlot dominated right bank – courtesy of the usual suspects, of course. And having retasted some left bank wines in October 2011 I am increasingly convinced of 2010's quality. Sadly though, this was a highly priced vintage from the outset. Nevertheless, these wines are going to be talked about for many, many years to come.

Bordeaux 2009

his is one of the great vintages of the early 21st century. The growing season was characterised by a long summer of stable temperatures, with these conditions persisting right through harvest time. There were a few notable estates, however, that struggled. A handful lost a portion, or indeed the majority, of their crop to storms which battered the vines with hailstones the size of golf balls. Much of the damage affected 'lesser' vineyards in the Entre-Deux-Mers, but some vineyards in Bourg, Blaye and St Emilion were also badly hit. Production at Château Trottevieille, for example, was just 700 cases for the entire vintage.

The uncharacteristically warm and dry harvest months made for comfortable picking but also threatened high sugar, alcohol and/or tannin levels. The ultimate challenge in this vintage was deciding when to pick; the point at which the fruit is harvested often depends on a battle of wills, with the technical directors of the leading Bordeaux châteaux on one side, and the vagaries of autumnal weather on the other. Generally, as harvest approaches the managers and proprietors watch the weather forecast and skies above, hoping to eke out a few more days of ripeness in the fruit. Eventually they crack, and the threat of rain forces the pickers into the fields. The 2009 vintage didn't provide this tipping point though, and the managers and directors had to send the team out based purely on analyses and tasting. In the majority of cases I suspect (from having tasted

WINES TO BUY

As is the case with 2010, the prices of 2009 Bordeaux take it largely out of reach. That's why I'm recommending some wines that are, hopefully, more affordable.

A Top Five for Realists
- Grand Puy Lacoste
- Rauzan-Ségla
- Domaine de Chevalier
- Branaire Ducru
- Saint-Pierre

Bordeaux on a Budget
- Gloria
- Sociando-Mallet
- Les Carmes Haut-Brion
- De Fieuzal
- Moulin-Saint-Georges

the wines) this went well, especially on the left bank, but I fear there was not such rigorous self-control at one or two right bank estates, and as a result there are a handful of wines where the tannins and alcohol have run amok.

Nevertheless, there's no denying this is a great vintage. Although we didn't know it at the time, it was the first of a vintage pair, as 2010 was equally prodigious, although in style the two are polar opposites. The 2009 wines are big, lush, textured and hedonistic. They have great structure, layers of tannin and fresh acidity, but such is the weight of the velvety blackcurrant, cherry, vanilla and creamy fruit placed on top, that these lower layers are often difficult to spot. Nevertheless the necessary structural elements, both tannin and acidity, are there. There is no doubt these are remarkable wines that will age very well, and will provide a unique drinking experience in years to come.

Bordeaux 2008

For much of the growing season it looked as though 2008 was going to be a re-run of 2007 – disappointing. The vines saw an early and irregular budbreak, leading to irregular fruit development. Spring frosts damaged some buds, and this was followed by a cool, damp summer. As with 2007 there was a persistent threat of rot and mildew (in general prevented by the spraying of chemicals) and a stuttering veraison (the change in colour from green to a ripe blue-black). However, a miraculous recovery ensued, and warm weather in September and October saved the vintage. Many harvests ran into October, and many Sauternes estates were still bringing in their fruit in November.

There are some excellent wines from most appellations in this vintage, which is far superior to 2007, but ultimately it can't hold a candle to the 2009 and 2010 vintages that followed. The right bank yielded more consistent success than the left, but that's not to say the Médoc is devoid of good wines – a handful thrill. But

the right bank produced breathtaking wines, from the leading estates right down to the less exalted names. The wines of Pomerol are slightly superior to those of St Emilion, but there's little in it. Overall they possess rich fruit, good acidity and, in the best examples, vibrant aromatics too.

As for the left bank, there is (occasionally) success here too. But whereas the right bank wines have dark fruits, richness, depth and, in some cases, considerable power, the left bank provides more vibrancy, more red fruit character and firmer acidities. This is not universal though; St Julien has the greatest success, showing lots of sweet summer berry fruit backed up by crisp acidity and ripe tannins. Paulliac also produced good wines, although with less purity than in St Julien. In Margaux the story is more patchy, but Palmer (see page 59) is brilliant. St Estèphe was less exciting, as were the wines of the Médoc and Haut-Médoc. This is not a vintage to wantonly scoop up left bank petits vins without tasting, purchasers will need to do their homework.

WINES TO BUY

This is a vintage for concentrating on the right bank appellations of St Emilion, Pomerol and beyond. Some second wines, such as Petit Cheval (from Cheval Blanc) and Chapelle d'Ausone (from Ausone) were divine, but are now very expensive. My top five focuses on more reasonably priced wines. On the left bank St Julien and Pauillac are strongest.

Right Bank: A Top Five for Realists
- Figeac
- Canon-la-Gaffelière
- Troplong-Mondot
- Latour à Pomerol
- Clos Fourtet

Left Bank: A Top Five for Realists
- Alter Ego de Palmer
- Domaine de Chevalier
- Branaire-Ducru
- Langoa-Barton
- Lagrange

Bordeaux 2007

Superficially at least, the story of 2007 reads rather like that of 2008. The 2007 growing season was characterised by an early but irregular budbreak, flowering and ripening that required a lot of work in the vineyard. The summer was, on the whole, rather cool and drizzly, delaying ripening, encouraging disease and requiring even more work in the vineyard. There was an ever-present threat of oidium and mildew, and not everybody was quick enough in the treating of these maladies. And yet, when all hope seemed dashed, warm weather in September brought a recovery. Or enough of a recovery, at least, to enable wine makers to produce a palatable beverage.

Twenty years ago this vintage would have been an undrinkable disaster, but modern methods meant that palatable wines were plucked from the jaws of the distillery. However, many wines are not great, in fact a large number are unremarkable early drinkers, yet it's fair to say

that amongst the rubble there are also a few very good wines to be found. Many are problematic though; there is greenness in some wines, and over-extraction in others. Even at my first taste it was clear that a large number of wines showed very bare structure through the midpalate, with no flesh to cover the tannins and acidity; some were overtly hollow and washed out, and many had a short finish to complete the picture. My most recent tasting in 2011 confirmed my earlier thoughts; this is a vintage of wines that are only 'decent'. They would make good early drinkers (for the restaurant trade, perhaps?) if they were priced appropriately. Unfortunately they tend not to be, the release prices were overly ambitious, and the wines are (largely) not worth the money.

One region that bucks this trend, however, is Sauternes. The wines, upon release, impressed with their crystalline fruit and deliciously evocative, vivacious aromas and flavours. Not many of the wines showed much overt botrytis-related aromas or texture, most being purer, linear and lightly golden in style, imbued with the aromas of mangoes, pineapples and peaches. Tasting more recently, however, the wines are revealing their botrytis depth more clearly, and seem to have the weight to match their acidity. My early declaration, that this was (before 2011 came along) the best Sauternes vintage since 2001, seems to have been proved correct.

WINES TO BUY

This is not a vintage to chase the red wines; they are largely overpriced. But if you have a penchant for dry white Bordeaux, or Sauternes and Barsac, then this is a vintage for you.

Top Ten Affordable Wines for Sauternes Realists

- Coutet
- Suduiraut
- Lafaurie-Peyraguey
- Doisy-Daëne
- Nairac
- Doisy-Védrines
- La Tour Blanche
- Guiraud
- Rieussec
- Sigalas-Rabaud

Bordeaux 2006

I t was inevitable after the success of 2005 that any hint of good weather during the 2006 growing season would lead to predictions of another great vintage, a 'double whammy'. And indeed, early on, 2006 certainly looked very promising. Dry weather meant the vines were restrained in their growth, only putting out a small number of bunches. This was further compounded by a summer heat wave, bringing incredibly warm temperatures and drought to May, June and July, and as a result hopes were raised – perhaps there really was another 2005 on the way? Sadly not, as it turned out. The heat of July was replaced by a cool, damp August, and all hopes were dashed. The grapes were swollen, rot ensued, the ripening was uneven and as a consequence some estates were out picking before full phenolic ripeness had been attained. All of these factors contributed towards the final quality – or lack of it – in the vintage.

Despite this, 2006 turned out to be a surprisingly successful year for the Bordelais and, provided you can stomach the price tags, there are plenty of appealing wines to be found here, on both banks of the Gironde. Looking across the entire region we have wines that are superior to

WINES TO BUY

Rather like in 2008, this is a vintage where the right bank appellations of St Emilion and Pomerol deserve our attention, hence I have pulled an 'affordable' – as much as that is possible – selection from these appellations, along with five wines for realists from the left bank.

Right Bank: A Top Five for Realists
- Beau-Séjour Becot
- Clos Fourtet
- Gazin
- Feytit-Clinet
- Monbousquet

Left Bank: A Top Five for Realists
- Domaine de Chevalier
- Smith Haut Lafitte
- Grand Puy Lacoste
- D'Armailhac
- Sociando-Mallet

those produced in 2007. This is no great surprise of course, as the latter was the most difficult year for the Bordelais since the disastrous vintages of the early 1990s. More importantly perhaps, I found wines that were superior to those from the 2008 vintage, although in many cases quality was very close. Ultimately it is style rather than quality that really sets the two vintages apart.

All this means is that from the trio of vintages that lie between the exorbitantly priced 2005 at one end, and the ultra-exorbitantly priced 2009 at the other, it is 2007 that should be avoided (unless the wines come down to a price approximating their true quality...which isn't likely) and we should look to a mix of 2006 (especially Pessac-Léognan and the right bank) and 2008 (especially St Julien and again the right bank) for some of the best wines.

Bordeaux 2005

Although the 2009 and 2010 vintages have received a great deal of positive press recently, if I were forced to choose one vintage from the past ten years it would be – at least until I've explored the 2010 vintage further – 2005. This was a vintage where the weather made the wine, while the winemakers relaxed. The summer saw warm but not excessively hot temperatures which did not overly stress the vines but instead helped the fruit towards perfect development. Ripening was both rapid and even, the fruit showing good flavour but also freshness and acidity, in the red grapes at least. These were small and nicely packed, with hard skins rich in tannin. Thus there was from the outset the potential for plenty of structure in the wines, as well as ripe substance, flavour and acidity. Although the permitted yields were very similar to those for 2004, the actual yields at harvest were considerably smaller than the previous year, testament to those small, concentrated, flavour-rich berries.

I have returned to these wines several times since the fruit was harvested; and have yet to be disappointed. There was, of course, not universal success, and a handful of wines have shown a little coarseness of tannin, or a confected edge to the fruit, but most taste wonderful, and even those that fail to exhibit the finest of characteristics still have much potential, as the tannins fade and the flavour profile develops over time. And we should

WINES TO BUY

Wines for Realists
Ten worthwhile wines that might not break the bank as they mature
- Grand-Mayne
- Cantemerle
- Prieuré-Lichine
- Monbrison
- Saint-Pierre
- Lagrange
- D'Armailhac
- Lafon-Rochet
- Brown
- Malartic-Lagravière

remember not to knock such great wines simply because they do not quite attain our idea of absolute perfection.

This is not only a vintage for great wines, but also for great value too. At the top end we have wines of supreme elegance, but there are also wines here which offer super value for money, right from the petits-châteaux making generic Bordeaux, up to the lower rungs of the cru classé châteaux. If you bought at the right time (the wines are inevitably more expensive now) it was possible to fill your cellar with wonderful wines, without breaking the bank.

Bordeaux 2004

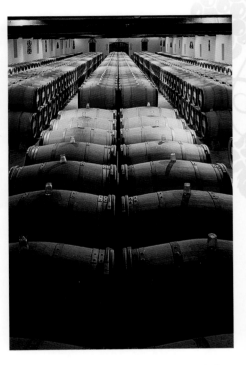

The 2004 vintage was not a particularly memorable one. Both 2002 and 2003 were at least distinctive, although in different ways – one crisp and fresh, and the other sun-baked. Nevertheless, it is a vintage worth knowing about. The wines may not be supreme, but neither are they grand disappointments. And they were, in many cases at least, favourably priced; although release prices were clearly on the up, the increments were nothing like those of the following years.

The growing season started off slowly, and flowering was late, pushing back (and therefore endangering) the eventual harvest. Not since 1988 had the harvest been so far into autumn. The vines were full of vigour, and the season would have permitted a huge crop which the vines would have tried (and probably failed) to ripen adequately. Pruning, green harvesting and good vineyard management was paramount. Ultimately, at harvest, some grapes were riper than others, although generally the Merlots tended to be in a better condition than the Cabernets. Nevertheless, there was some rain before harvest, and not all grapes had recovered

from their swollen state before being picked; there was plenty of opportunity to maximise the quality of the wine with both careful selection, and handling, in the cellar.

There was no real star performance from any particular commune in this vintage, so it is more a question of carefully picking and choosing from across the board. As the wines approach maturity there is plenty of good value to be found. My list to the left highlights a number of leading estates absent – on the basis of high price – from lists of more recent, more exalted vintages. If there is one feature of 2004 we should be grateful for, it is the fact that prices still reflect the quality of the wine, and that the vintage pre-dates the worst of the most ambitious pricing to come out of Bordeaux in recent years.

WINES TO BUY

Wines for Realists

Ten worthwhile wines that might not break the bank as the wines mature

- Rauzan-Ségla
- Giscours
- Langoa Barton
- Grand Puy Lacoste
- Léoville-Poyferré
- Léoville-Barton
- Gazin
- Beauregard
- Grand Mayne
- Clos Fourtet

Bordeaux 2003

I f there is a lead contender for most unusual vintage of recent years, then 2003 must surely be it (although 2011 is shaping up as a serious contender). The first signs that this vintage might be out of the ordinary came in late March, when warm, dry weather prompted vigorous growth and early budbreak. But it was the sweltering summer months of June and July, followed by an August roasting, that really set the Bordeaux 2003 vintage apart. Temperatures in the latter month regularly exceeded 40C, an unprecedented event in the region. The heat wave, which saw three weeks where no rain touched the soils of Bordeaux, placed a significant hardship on the vines, and despite the presence of deep water many vines shut down photosynthesis in response to the stress. Such heat also has a direct effect on

the berries, roasting and hardening the skins. Low acidity, the levels depleted by such tumultuously hot weather, was another concern.

The low acidities were said to climb during fermentation, although many wines don't seem to display this now. The grapes were roasted and thick-skinned, bringing the possibility of roasted flavours and, most importantly, undesirable tannins. All-in-all there has always been good reason for viewing the wines of this vintage with a very cautious, circumspect eye.

Many years down the road it is clear that terroir was vital in determining how the vines coped with the onslaught of 2003. The appellation with the best reputation in this vintage is St Estèphe, with its clay, moisture-retaining soils. Elsewhere, St Emilion – which has a similar terroir – also yielded some surprisingly good wines. But areas such as Pessac-Léognan which are richer in gravel, and where the vines suffered most, yielded wines which in many cases are already showing their age. Finally, don't shy away from the sweet wines of this year; although a hot, baked vintage is not one that intuitively suggests great sweet wines will be made (the dry weather discouraging botrytis, and the heat lowering the much-needed balancing acidity), there are still some brilliant Sauternes available in this vintage.

WINES TO BUY

Wines for Realists
Five worthwhile wines that might not break the bank as they mature
- Bellevue
- Lafon-Rochet
- Troplong-Mondot
- Langoa-Barton
- Canon la Gaffelière

Five Sauternes worth considering
- Coutet
- Rieussec
- Nairac
- Doisy-Védrines
- Suduiraut

2

News from The Region

You might think – having glanced at the 1855 classification of Bordeaux – that Bordeaux as a region is stuck in, and obsessed with, the past. Don't let this superficial impression fool you; Bordeaux is as dynamic a region as any other, with new blood arriving, new acquisitions being made, and new wines waiting to be discovered. This section of my Bordeaux guide deals with the most newsworthy developments in recent times from across the region.

Latour withdraw from en primeur

I n a significant development in the story of Bordeaux, technical director Frédéric Engerer informed négociants in April 2012 that the 2011 vintage would be the last time Latour would be sold en primeur.

From the 2012 vintage onwards Latour will not be released en primeur, or even once the wine has just gone into bottle. Instead the wines will be held back by the château in new, purpose-built cellars, and not offered to the market until they approach their drinking window. What this means is open to interpretation, but I expect we will see vintages come onto the market at 6-10 years of age. It is not quite a first for Bordeaux (Château Gilette in Sauternes releases only mature wines), nevertheless this is an unprecedented step for a château of Latour's pedigree. This is a huge change for Latour, and for Bordeaux.

What knock-on effect

will this have? It may lessen the interest in the en primeur market, especially if other first growths follow suit, but less financially capable châteaux will not be able to follow them. If the primeurs lose the support of big guns such as Latour, it may well falter, and this could cause great difficulties for smaller châteaux. And all those who make their money off Bordeaux – the négociants in France, and the merchants across the world – will also take a financial hit. There could be big changes ahead for Bordeaux and the primeurs.

Carmenère Returns to Bordeaux

I n late 2011 I visited Château Brane-Cantenac, and finished up my visit there with a sneaky taste of an experimental cuvée, a sample of Carmenère, a grape today mostly commonly associated with Chile but which originated in Bordeaux. It is a fickle creature, and tends to ripen late (historically a problem in this cool-climate region), and so it fell out of favour with local producers. But in these days of climate change late-ripening is less of a problem, and keen to obtain some new experience with the variety the team at Brane-Cantenac planted an experimental 0.5-hectare plot in 2007. The 2011 harvest was only the third (it takes two or three years before

the vines bear fruit) and the quality is already good enough for the variety to earn its place in the Brane-Cantenac 2011 grand vin.

"Welcome back Carmenère," is the cry from many in Bordeaux, although perhaps not from Paul Pontallier, the erudite and scientifically minded director of Château Margaux. At a London tasting of Margaux experimental wines (including wines under screwcap, and from biodynamic plots) held in early 2012 he was heard to say that a good Carmenère "is less rustic than a bad one". I don't think we will be seeing this prodigal grape variety making an appearance in Pontallier's vineyards any time soon!

China Moves to Bordeaux

It's no great news that China's appetite for Bordeaux has grown massively in the last few years. But whereas once they were happy importing, buying and drinking the wines, it seems that now they're looking to get involved at the coal-face, so to speak. Rather than Bordeaux going to China, China is now coming to Bordeaux, and the past year has seen a string of châteaux sold to wealthy Chinese buyers. One typical example was Laulan-Ducos which was acquired by TESiRO, a jewelry business, early in 2011. Frédéric Ducos had been struggling to find new markets for his wine for some time, despite good quality, and was perhaps relieved to find a buyer for the family business. He has stayed on to work for the new owners, and with new investment expects Laulan-Ducos to become – in his words – "a big luxury brand in China." Other châteaux now in Chinese hands include Château Monlot in St Emilion (bought in December 2011 by actress Zhao Wei and husband Huang Youlong, reportedly for more than €4 million) and Château Lezongars (also sold in December 2011, for an undisclosed sum), and there are at least half a dozen more. In some cases, these were châteaux that had been languishing on the market for quite a while, and I suspect new investment from wealthy owners might be exactly what is needed. And China provides a ready market – a win-win situation.

And Bordeaux Moves to China

A key player in China's growing love for Bordeaux has been Château Lafite-Rothschild, whose wine now sells for many times what it realised ten years ago thanks to the Chinese appetite for it. Even the second wine, Carruades de Lafite, now fetches prices that many proprietors of Bordeaux châteaux can only dream of, so it's no surprise that the leading players in Bordeaux should court this affluent and growing market. Whether it is to conduct a special auction of their wines, or to host a tasting dinner atop the Great Wall of China, Hong Kong and mainland China are now regular destinations for the directors of some of Bordeaux's top châteaux.

The next step is, naturally, establishing vineyards in China. The grape vine is in fact no stranger to this country, as was proven when a Chinese wine picked up a trophy at the 2011 Decanter World Wine Awards, in the Bordeaux category no less. But bolstered by the success of Lafite in China the Rothschild family have gone one further than everybody else, and in 2012 the foundations were laid for their new Chinese winery in Penglai, a well-established viticultural region. Only time will tell what quality these wines will display, but one thing is for sure. The Chinese appetite for all things Lafite seems likely to become even stronger.

Lascombes Under the Hammer

Although China's voracious appetite for Bordeaux seems only likely to increase, and they are even buying châteaux in the region, most acquisitions have been rather low-key, and tended to focus on lesser appellations such as the Entre-Deux-Mers or Médoc. The acquisition of a classed growth château by a Chinese buyer has yet to happen, although many seem to think it inevitable…at some stage.

In the meantime, one or two other châteaux have changed hands in the past year. First of these is Château Lascombes, an estate that was rescued from a long period in the doldrums when it was acquired by Capital Colony back in 2001. It had been rumoured for quite some time that the château was on the market – and when your owner is a huge private real estate investment firm looking for a strong return, it is probably true to say that – for the right price – you are always for sale. The sale to Mutuelle d'Assurances du Corps de Santé Français (or MACSF for those with limited time), a French pensions group, in July 2011 didn't cause too many eyebrows to rise. It was perhaps the price that was the most newsworthy element of the story. The estate was sold for €200 million (including stock valued at €50 million – a figure no doubt bolstered by the very high prices set by the Lascombes team for the 2009 and 2010 vintages), which was a 300% increase on the acquisition price in 2001.

Haut-Brion Branch Out

Perhaps the other big item of acquisitions news in during 2011/2012 has been the purchase of Château Tertre Daugay in St Emilion by Domaine Clarence Dillon, better known as the proprietor of Château Haut-Brion and Château La Mission Haut-Brion in Pessac-Léognan. Prince Robert of Luxembourg, head of Domaine Clarence Dillon, and his estate manager Jean-Philippe Delmas have been busy restructuring the Haut-Brion portfolio in recent years, waving goodbye to Latour Haut-Brion (now absorbed into the second wine of La Mission) and renaming wines (Laville Haut-Brion became the white wine of La Mission Haut-Brion, to offer but one example). One has to assume that, having finished with this flurry of new nomenclature, they decided it was time to look further afield for a new project.

They acquired Château Tertre-Daugay in June 2011, although much of the world's wine press only became aware of this significant development with the arrival of a glossy press release, which came through the post in early 2012. The property is widely regarded as having significant unexploited potential, having maintained an extremely high reputation during the 19th century. In keeping with the recent Clarence Dillon trend for renaming wines, the estate has been rebranded Château Quintus, and I hope to be able to report on the fruit of the château's labour later this year. I can't wait to see how the estate progresses.

New Cellars...

With the profits pouring in from the highly priced 2009 and 2010 vintages Bordeaux has perhaps never been in such a strong financial position. Many of Bordeaux's châteaux have disappeared behind facades of scaffolding and tarpaulin in recent years, as aged stonework is cleaned, repointed and refurbished. Some have gone one step further though, and where considered appropriate simply levelled the 'château' and started again.

In the first camp is Château Cheval Blanc, one of the leading domaines in St Emilion, sitting pretty at the top of the St Emilion classification alongside the smaller-scale Château Ausone. This property is now blessed with stunning new cellars, designed by architect Christian de Portzamparc, which were unveiled in July 2011. The new facilities are filled with the latest equipment, including rows of custom-built temperature-controlled cement vats.

In the second camp is superstar Le Pin, a Pomerol first growth (or it would be if such a classification existed). Having visited Le Pin several times I was always taken by the disconnect between the extraordinarily high prices fetched by the wine, and the tumble-down nature of the little house that overlooked the vineyard, with its peeling paint and crumbling façade. However, this has now been replaced by a rather blocky and minimalist building which sits atop sizeable, space-age cellars.

...and New Rooms

While not quite displaying the curvaceous lines of the new cellars at Cheval Blanc, or the more futuristic appearance of Le Pin, Château Lagrange in St Julien is still a sight worth seeing, a traditional Bordeaux château complemented by the addition of an Italianate tower which seems, for all the world, to have been plucked directly from some Tuscan town and dropped in Bordeaux. And visitors who fall in love with the château can now indulge themselves with a stay at the property itself, in one of the recently refurbished rooms available to rent.

On behalf of the owners, the Japanese wine and spirits company Suntory, the estate's director Bruno Ebrard has overseen the upgrading of guest rooms to meet the demands of modern tourists and visitors to Bordeaux. There are 14 bedrooms, all unveiled during 2011, as well as a fully renovated and equipped tasting room. Outside Bordeaux, accommodation in the heart of the Médoc vineyards can be difficult to come by (there are some hotels, but not many) so this development will be a very popular one I'm sure.

Prices go Higher and Higher…

Any suspicions that the 2009 vintage was over-priced on release, and that prices would ultimately collapse, seem to have been squashed in early 2012 with the release of Robert Parker's scores for the vintage. Having retasted the wines, he pronounced 19 of the wines to be perfect, anointing them with his top score, 100 points. Several newcomers to the 100-point club were featured in the list, names such as Château Clinet, Château Smith-Haut-Lafitte and Clos Fourtet.

Without a doubt Parker's scores are the strongest driver of acute price fluctuations in the aftermarket, and the prices of all the 100-point wines unsurprisingly went up after the announcement was made. Big movers included Clos Fourtet and Smith-Haut-Lafitte (both up by more than 130%), Beauséjour Duffau Lagarosse (about a 100% increase here), and even Pontet-Canet – already much sought after – increased in value by over 30%.

Curiously, once the new prices were released availability didn't seem to be a problem, leading some to suggest new stock had been placed on the market after the prices had risen. Although unsubstantiated, this would fit with the belief held by many that large amounts of stock were held back in 2009 and 2010 in order to restrict supply and maintain the highest prices ever. The business of selling Bordeaux lacks transparency, and so we will never know if this is true or not…but all the new buildings going up along the Médoc must be for storing something, surely?

…and Higher Still

It's not just the 2009 vintage that is characterised by sky-high prices, some older vintages also have the potential to break the bank. Although, considering how superior Bordeaux becomes with appropriate age, it is very strange that so many mature wines are available at lower prices than younger vintages. One favoured vintage is 1961, one of the greatest years of the 20th century, correctly ranked alongside 1945 and 1982. And in May 2011 a single bottle of wine from this vintage went under the hammer and sold for £135,000 in Hong Kong (where else, but the wine world's new power-house for wine auctions). Admittedly, it was a six-litre bottle – otherwise known as an Impériale – but the price is still impressive. The wine was sold by Christie's, and it is reported to have gone to a Chinese bidder.

Not Just China (1)

I t's not just China that is interested in acquiring a foothold in Bordeaux; other nations have a taste for the wine too. Russia is another increasingly important player, with several Bordeaux châteaux having been snapped up in recent years by Russian buyers. Clos Dady in Sauternes is one of the latest to change hands, having been purchased by Muscovite Ilkham Ragimov back in November 2011. A modest 6-hectare estate, Clos Dady was secured by Ragimov for the sum of €1.5 million, and the sale also included three hectares of vines outside the Sauternes appellation. Ragimov has reportedly struck a deal with Jerome Cosson and Audrey Fargues of nearby Chateau d'Arche to make the wine on his behalf.

Of course, Russia has a rather longer association with wine than China, and indeed with Sauternes, which does not seem to have broken through in China yet. This is despite the best efforts of proprietors such as Jean-Pierre Meslier, of Château Raymond-Lafon, who told me in late 2011 he was actively looking to sell more wine in Asian markets. And so it is perhaps not so much of a surprise to see Russian investment here. Nevertheless, they lag behind the Chinese, with the only really notable acquisition beyond Clos Dady being Château Livran, in the Médoc appellation.

Not Just China (2)

T he artistic works that have graced the labels of Château Mouton-Rothschild since the 1945 vintage (following the Jean Carlu label, which first appeared on the 1924 vintage) have come from all manner of artists, from Andy Warhol to Joan Miró. But with Asian markets developing at a great pace, sceptics were not surprised to see a Chinese artist selected for the 2008 vintage. Xu Lei is famed for combining Chinese ink and brush techniques with Western surrealism, and his label for the 2008 is in keeping with this work.

But it's not just China; step forward Anish Kapoor, a British artist of Indian descent best known for his imposing works of sculpture such as the Unilever Commission at the Tate Modern in London. Kapoor has been selected as the artist for the 2009 label. As yet, India is not a great market for Bordeaux but there is undoubtedly growing interest in wine there, and serious financial potential. Perhaps the team at Mouton-Rothschild know something we don't?

Chinese Names Approved...and Denied

No wine region gets away without the occasional farce, and Bordeaux is no exception. The scene for Bordeaux's latest controversy – involving China (again) – was set in February 2012 when Christie's published what they claimed was an official translation of the names of the remaining 61 châteaux in the 1855 classification. Decanter reported that Simon Tam, head of wine in China for Christie's said "We have written confirmation and agreements from all but three or four châteaux that these Chinese translations are the agreed names for the whole Chinese speaking world." Clearly, the auction house hoped to take the credit for providing the wine trade with a definitive list of Chinese names.

Unfortunately, Christie's ended up with egg on their face when, just one week later, they appeared to have landed themselves in the middle of a storm in a Bordeaux teacup. The Conseil des Grands Crus Classés en 1855, as well as a number of relevant châteaux, all refused to have anything to do with the list, and denied having approved the "official" translations. Nevertheless, Tam and Christie's elected to ignore this backlash; after all, they already had 500 copies of the poster, detailing the translations, printed in readiness for the 2011 primeur tastings in Bordeaux.

A Farcical Fine

Finally, I couldn't resist bringing you news of this story concerning rocketing sales of sugar in a small, provincial grocery store in Sainte Croix du Mont, a region known for its sweet wines (found just across the river from Sauternes). Granulated sugar might not have much to do with wine, you might think, but in fact the opposite is true; it is legal in many French appellations to add sugar to the fermenting wine, to increase the alcohol concentration. These days quality-orientated growers eschew such practices, but less scrupulous growers don't. The quantity which can be added is limited by law, though, and sales must be regulated, documented and taxed.

Which is perhaps why Therese Solano's corner shop was so popular; over two years she sold over 150 tonnes of sugar, keeping neither a record of the purchaser, or any receipts. The sales tended to spike at harvest time, although in Solano's defence she says she thought her customers were making jam. Enough jam to need 150 tonnes of sugar? Demand was especially high in 2007, apparently, obviously a good year for jam-making...but coincidentally a rather poor year for red wine, when barely ripe grapes meant the fermenting wines would benefit from a sugar boost. Solano was prosecuted, and received a €5000 fine in November 2011.

2011 Vintage Review

3

The growing season of 2011 was certainly a challenging one for Bordeaux. Spring was remarkably warm, but spirits were dampened (as were the vines) by a prolonged spell of cool and wet weather during the summer. As many of the Bordelais told me during my visits to the region last October, and again in April to taste the young barrel samples, "summer was spring, and spring was summer," the first drier and warmer than usual, the second cooler and wetter. There were other problems too. June saw a mini heat wave during the final week of the month which damaged some of the fruit. Thereafter there were lower than expected temperatures through the summer months, and during heavy rain in August many estates deleafed to help increase the exposure of the fruit, both to encourage ripening and improve ventilation in damp conditions. Although an appropriate response at the time, this only caused further problems later in the year. In addition, some vineyards were hit by hail.

The Merlots are always picked first, starting on September 5th last year, and a number of estates with good records told me this was their earliest harvest since 1893. The Cabernets ripen later and were left on the vine for one or two weeks more, the earliest official harvest being September 12th (some hail-struck vineyards in St Estèphe were harvested earlier). Without the protection of the leaf canopy (following the summer deleafing) and with warm and dry weather, these berries suffered from dehydration. The grapes shriveled, developing a high skin-to-juice ratio and thus a high concentration of

tannins. As far as the red wines go the main issues that determined quality were (a) rigorous selection in order to weed out damaged, unripe, shriveled or rotten berries, and (b) sensitive extraction of tannins in the winery. Otherwise there was plenty of potential for making poor wines, dominated by drying or chewy tannins.

Indeed, in this most unusual of vintages we have all quality levels. Those that rushed out to pick too soon, for whatever reason – hail, rain, rot or otherwise – have made green and dilute wines. Those that left it too late harvested raisined fruit and made pruney wines. You can find all styles of wine, in all appellations, in this vintage. But those that got it right – harvesting correctly ripe fruit, with rigorous selection and sensitive extraction – made good wines. Even at the top level, though, the wines are not comparable with 2009 or 2010, two vintages which have sold (not so well in the case of the latter) at escalated prices. Very careful selection for buying will be required for 2011. In general, the wines will not be worth buying en primeur, unless there are huge cuts in release prices in order to generate interest.

LEFT BANK: FIVE TOP PICKS

Pauillac was one of the stronger communes on the left bank in 2011:

- Montrose
- Lafite-Rothschild
- Pichon-Baron
- Pontet-Canet
- Mouton-Rothschild

LEFT BANK: VALUE PICKS

Five left-bank wines which, depending on the release price, should offer the most for your money:

- Tronquoy-Lalande
- Gloria
- Pibran
- Cantemerle
- Batailley

The Left Bank: Commune by Commune

St Estèphe endured as much as any other commune this year, plus a little bit more, having been the victim of a devastating hailstorm which cut a path across the vineyards on September 1st 2011. It took out a number of notable vineyards, its most significant victim being Cos d'Estournel, although all in the locality suffered to some extent. Vines belonging to Lafon-Rochet and Cos Labory were affected, and smaller and less significant areas of the Montrose, Haut-Marbuzet and Phélan-Ségur vineyards were also hit. Despite this both Montrose and Cos d'Estournel have turned out excellent wines this year; the rest of the commune hasn't faired so well, though.

Pauillac is stronger than St Estèphe in 2011, and one of the best wines comes from Pichon Baron, where technical director Christian Seely stated that understanding the vintage meant "having a light hand" when it came to extraction,

as I have already explained in my vintage review. Those that extracted too hard and thereby made overly tannic and drying wines "have missed the personality of the year," says Seely. Other excellent wines can be found at Pontet-Canet, even though the biodynamic Tesserons seem to have bucked the trend for hard selection in this vintage by channeling 90% of their harvest into the grand vin. Lafite is rich but linear and fine, whereas Mouton shows all the seductive spice that typify the wines of this estate. Some wines are very good indeed, but many are robustly tannic.

Moving on to St Julien Léoville-Barton is, for me, the superior of the three Léoville wines this year (and the best in the appellation). Whereas some wines of the commune display rather exotic flavours and voluptuous flesh, Léoville-Barton is restrained and classically styled. And yet there is plenty of substance here too, and the tannins prove full and convincing. The oft-reliable Langoa-Barton, unsurprisingly, displayed the same style and polish upon my tasting it. Other sterling efforts were made by the team at Saint-Pierre and Gloria. At the other end of the quality spectrum comes Léoville-Poyferré, a massively extracted wine which lacks balance. Nevertheless St Julien is perhaps the most consistent left-bank commune, even if Pauillac

CHAPTER THREE

RIGHT BANK: FIVE TOP PICKS

It is a vintage where, in these communes (unlike the left bank) the best wines come from the estates of long-standing recognition, with a strong focus on Pomerol:

- Petrus
- Lafleur (and Pensées de Lafleur)
- Vieux Château Certan
- Trotanoy
- Lafleur-Pétrus

ultimately achieves greater highs.

In Margaux there are not many wines for us to concern ourselves with. By far the best is from Palmer, which knocks spots off Margaux itself...an estate where Paul Pontallier has made an undeniably good wine, but one that, ultimately, falls short of what I was hoping for from the first growth estate. Palmer has paid a high price to gain such quality though, with the lowest recorded yield here since the fabled 1961 vintage, and only 20% of the harvest going into the grand vin. Beyond these two good wines the appellation is dogged by green, dilute and plain vegetal wines.

Pessac-Léognan

Speaking to Jean-Philippe Delmas of Haut-Brion and La Mission Haut-Brion in Pessac-Léognan, (and tasting his wines) it seemed clear that these properties – and indeed the whole of the appellation – has struggled in 2011. At the Dillon properties the ripeness of the fruit was very heterogeneous, each bunch carrying a mix of green, burnt and rotten grapes. All of these trouble-makers needed to be selected out in order to leave only the ripe and healthy fruit. For the

PESSAC-LÉOGNAN: FIVE PICKS

I don't feel compelled to recommend any of the red wines. From the whites:

- Domaine de Chevalier
- Smith-Haut-Lafitte
- Pape-Clément
- La Mission-Haut-Brion
- Brown

third time ever Jean-Philippe felt compelled to rent an optical sorter to improve selection.

Nevertheless despite these sterling efforts the wines are not as strong as they have been in recent vintages. The Haut-Brion and La Mission Haut-Brion wines in particular are no match for the 2010 and 2009, and the second wines are particularly weak. The 2011 vintage has been a very challenging one for Pessac-Léognan, as it is for the Margaux appellation on the other side of the city of Bordeaux. Looking specifically at reds, there are few good wines here. For my palate Haut-Bailly put in the best performance, with a decent effort from Smith-Haut-Lafitte also worth a mention. The whites though are delicious, fresh, fruit-rich, and full of lively acidity thanks to that cooler summer, with a good concentration.

Right Bank

On the right bank there are highs and lows, just as there are in some of the left bank communes. St Emilion is always a mixed bag, it being a commune with no strong stylistic identity. At the very top in this vintage we have some excellent wines; Ausone is beautifully tense and pure, with lots of structure tucked in underneath, and it should be a great wine given time. Its counterpart at the top of the St Emilion classification, Cheval Blanc, has a more supple and seductive style, but it is rich in fruit and highly polished, a triumph of winemaking. Could Pierre Lurton's new €15 milllion cellars, complete with bespoke cement fermentation vessels, each one linked to a specific plot in the vineyard, have something to do with that? There are plenty of other good wines though, with Beau-Séjour-Bécot a notable success, as well as Clos Fourtet.

Last but certainly not least, Pomerol is the

RIGHT-BANK: FIVE VALUE PICKS

St Emilion is well represented here, but keep an eye out for lower-priced Pomerols such as the two recommended:

- Beau-Séjour-Bécot
- Moulin-Saint-Georges
- Fonbel
- Petit Village (Pomerol)
- La Pointe (Pomerol)

strongest right-bank commune in this vintage, and perhaps the strongest of all red wine communes. At the top end, the wines are majestic, with no sign of the difficult tannins that plague wines more dependent on Cabernet Sauvignon. Petrus is in the lead, a tour de force in terms of combined strength and focus, but Vieux Château Certan and Lafleur make magnificent alternatives. Other less exalted properties have also turned out good wines although – as is the case in all the red wine appellations in this vintage – there are 'downs' as well as 'ups' even here.

Sauternes

The real superstars of 2011, eclipsing the reds and dry whites, are the sweet wines of Sauternes and Barsac. These wines depend on the concentrating effects of botrytis in the vineyards to push the sugar levels up, giving them their distinct textures and flavours, and 2011 was blessed with a prodigious wave of botrytis. Nevertheless, it was not an easy or straightforward vintage for the Sauternais. The most important job was to pick out all the fruit that had succumbed to grey rot, which is very detrimental, as opposed to the characteristic noble rot of botrytis. This grey rot was the result of rain in July and August, allowing the mould to proliferate, encouraged by warmer temperatures in early September. Slightly different weather conditions meant that this was more of an issue for Sauternes than it was for Barsac, as a sequence of storms swept over the region in late August/early September, the most significant of which missed Barsac.

Once this was done the Sauternais waited for the botrytis, and in early September it attacked. The harvest generally began around the same time that the Merlots were picked on the Médoc, around September 5th, very early for Sauternes. Some started later, perhaps as late as September 10th, particularly in Barsac. But on the whole picking was undertaken quickly, a response to the rapid onset of botrytis, with most of the fruit coming in from the 12th onwards in Barsac and between September 20th and 25th in Sauternes. Thus by the time I visited the region in mid-October – more or less the time of the harvest for the 2010 vintage – all the fruit had long been picked. It had been the earliest harvest ever, even earlier than the previously record-breaking 2003 harvest. Provided the early culling of grey rot in the vineyard was carried out correctly, the potential was there for some great wines.

Having been to Bordeaux to taste the wines myself, I was blown away by the quality of these wines. What really lifts them is their wonderful acidity; they have rich textures suggestive of plenty of botrytis, implying that these are wines set to develop wonderful flavours. But those cool and damp summer months have preserved the acidity in the fruit, giving them – despite some handsome residual sugars – wonderful balance, freshness and finesse. This is a great vintage for the sweet wines of the region, especially for drinkers who crave balance over mere power. Certainly, the best vintage since 2001.

SAUTERNES: TOP FIVE PICKS

These wines are magnificent, and even at such high prices offer great value considering the effort that lies behind them

- Yquem
- Coutet
- Suduiraut
- Doisy-Daëne
- Rieussec

SAUTERNES: VALUE PICKS

For those shopping on a budget, however, these wines are – depending on the release prices, of course – likely to offer value for money

- Raymond-Lafon
- Liot
- Myrat
- Cantegril
- Caillou

4

The Firsts

The first growths of the Médoc and Sauternes are now priced beyond the pocket of most of us, as are the leading wines of the right bank appellations of St Emilion and Pomerol. The only way to experience these wines, apart from winning the lottery, is to group together with wine interested friends to buy a bottle. Nevertheless, it is certainly worth the effort and expense; these are benchmark wines which define the region.

Château Latour

Best recent vintage: 2009
Also worth a look: 2008

This estate is ancient, although, as is the case with many of the Médoc communes, viticulture only really arrived here relatively recently, in this case during the 18th century. The estate has passed through many famous hands, including Marquis Nicolas-Alexandre de Ségur, otherwise known as the Prince des Vignes, Barton & Guestier, the négociant firm established by Hugh Barton and Daniel Guestier, and a portion also came in 1840 to Nathaniel Johnston, the merchant business established by William Johnston. Ownership during much of the 20th century was unsure, the estate eventually falling into the hands of Allied Lyons in 1989, and then in 1993 to the management of French billionaire François Pinault. Latour thus became part of a business portfolio which was later augmented by the addition of Gucci, Yves Saint Laurent and Christie's auction house. Rumours of a sale which did the rounds in late 2008 came to nothing, and Pinault remains in charge here to this day.

Pinault entrusts the day-to-day management of the property and vineyards to Frédéric Engerer, and together the two have been responsible for continued improvements to the estate. Needless to say, Latour hasn't been short-changed when it comes to investment and development over the last few years. Most recent is another renovation of the chai, it having been updated to a fabulous specification, and fully equipped with gleaming new equipment. In the vineyards Cabernet Sauvignon accounts for 80% of the vines. The remainder is mostly Merlot, planted wherever clay is more prominent, and then a splash of Cabernet Franc and Petit Verdot. Notably, 14 hectares are under biodynamic viticulture, and 6 hectares are organic. The wines made here include the grand vin, a notable second wine (Les Forts de Latour), and there is also a third wine, Pauillac de Latour.

For many, Château Latour is the epitome of claret. Many would regard it as the leading first growth, and in the eternal quest to find 'the wine of the vintage' it is frequently Latour that comes out on top. Indeed, when it came to the primeur tastings of the 2008 vintage, this was indeed how I ranked Latour, and in other recent vintages it has never been far from the top of the tree. The wine also has, as is fitting for a first growth, a phenomenal propensity for ageing well. Many tasters remark that the 1899, 1900, 1928, or perhaps the 1945 (or in fact any number of other vintages), rank high in their list of candidates for favourite Latour vintage.

> It is no secret Frédéric Engerer would like Latour to be the 'First of the Firsts', and with François Pinault's backing he may well succeed. A move to withdraw Latour from the en primeur sales, announced in May 2012, may prove a significant step towards this. See page 22.

Château Lafite-Rothschild

Best recent vintage: 2009
Also worth a look: 2005

While penning the Lafite-Rothschild château profile for this publication, it occurred to me I no longer knew whether I was writing about Lafite-Rothschild the wine producer, or Lafite-Rothschild the investment opportunity. Once 'merely' a superb estate responsible for the production of a very desirable wine (one that was ranked at the very top of the 1855 classification and for many the very epitome of Pauillac, if not all of Bordeaux) the Lafite-Rothschild of the 21st century is no longer 'just' a wine. Lafite is now many different things, to many different people. The first of the firsts is the darling of the Chinese, who have been buying the estate's wines with gusto. Some regard it not so much as a beverage, more as a luxury product akin to any highly priced designer brand, one where perhaps prestige takes precedence over substance. Others might think of it purely as an investment vehicle, there to be traded, bought and sold, hopefully turning a tidy profit in the process and contributing significantly toward one's

retirement fund, for example. Lafite is perhaps all these things but we should also not forget that – above all else – Lafite-Rothschild is still a wine.

The origins of the château lie in the 14th century, and as with so many of these exalted estates it has been passed down through the generations by many a different hand, although some familiar names do crop up, such as Nicolas-Alexandre de Ségur, a wealthy nobleman once known as the Prince des Vignes in the 18th century. Eventually though it came to the Rothschild family, bankers of considerable wealth, who acquired the estate in the late 19th century. It has been alleged that this purchase was purely born of jealousy, the buyer Baron James de Rothschild perhaps merely wanting to match (or indeed better) what his cousins were achieving at nearby Mouton-Rothschild. There is perhaps some truth in this, although I am sure the reasons for his purchase were broader sweeping than mere bitterness.

Latterly it is Baron Eric de Rothschild, and even more recently his managing director Charles Chevalier, who are due much of the credit for Lafite's renaissance. Following some difficult vintages in the 1960s and 1970s, the stage was set for a number of the excellent wines that appeared through the 1990s, as well as the opening vintages of the 21st century. What comes out of the estate each year is not only the grand vin but also the second wine, Carruades de Lafite. Thanks principally to demand from Asia, in recent years the value of the second wine climbed to levels previously undreamed of, far higher than most other wines of Bordeaux. Eventually this effect filtered down to the first wine, a bizarre order of events, and then onto many other wines from Bordeaux. Prices across the board are much, much higher than they once were, but it is Lafite that led the way in this respect.

Throughout 2011 the price of a single bottle of Carruades de Lafite has been in excess of £200 ($300/€250), a sum of money that would have been sufficient for a bottle of the first wine only a few years ago, or indeed an entire case of many other wines of Bordeaux.

Château Mouton-Rothschild

Best recent vintage: 2009
Also worth a look: 1996

Many famous artists have had their work used on the Mouton labels, from Andy Warhol to HRH Prince Charles. Their payment is reputedly five cases of the current vintage and five cases of older vintages – not a bad commission.

The uninitiated turning up to taste the latest vintage at one of the left bank's first growth estates, would be forgiven for expecting a unique experience, something a little different. Surprisingly, however, one or two of the world's greatest wine producers offer rather perfunctory tastings, so if you are adamant that you deserve a little extravagance then it is to Mouton-Rothschild you should go. Fine art adorns the waiting room, alongside ancient statuary. No need to walk to the tasting room, let the staff whisk you over in golf buggies. Revel in the decadence of the golden sculptures, giant gilt-framed mirrors and, should you boast the right connections, Baroness Philippine de Rothschild herself holding court. But let us not forget the wines (they are why we're here, after all), opulently seductive, full of Mouton spice, just like their very surroundings. Some of course will see it as gaudy and brash, a presentation lacking the decorum of a real premier grand cru classé, a reference to Mouton's elevation from second to first growth by ministerial decree in 1973, 118 years after the 1855 classification was drawn up.

Like Lafite this estate has ancient origins and has had many owners, meaning it did not come into the hands of the Rothschilds until it was acquired by Baron Nathaniel de Rothschild in 1853. It has remained in the hands of this family ever since, perhaps the most significant member to hold the reins being Philippe Rothschild. It was he who introduced domaine bottling, rather than selling the wine in barrel, and he also introduced Mouton's famous artist labels, featuring a design by cubist Jean Carlu for the 1924 vintage. He was also the driving force behind the ultimately successful campaign to have Mouton elevated to first growth status.

Today the wines are made by Philippe Dhalluin, and include the grand vin as well as a second wine Le Petit Mouton, introduced in 1993, and also a white wine Aile d'Argent. The vineyards he works with are 80% Cabernet Sauvignon, 10% Cabernet Franc, 8% Merlot and 2% Petit Verdot, and present also is Sauvignon Blanc, Semillon and Muscadelle for the estate's white wine. The wines, thinking particularly of the first wine, are very distinctive, with a lush character and rich, individual spice to them. Not every vintage is fabulous – I certainly have some disappointing memories of the 1993 and 1994 – but more recently, especially since the arrival of Dhalluin in 2003, quality has been pushed higher and higher, with the selection of fruit for the grand vin seemingly stricter with every vintage.

Château Margaux

Best recent vintage: 2010
Also worth a look: 1996

Of all the first growths, Margaux is certainly a strong contender for being the most splendidly presented, its imposing 19th-century château, which peers over the chai, barrel cellars and other buildings easily visible from the D2, the road that snakes up the Médoc past the front doors of many of the classed growths. It stands proud, surrounded by sweeping rows of vines, the only visual challenge coming from Château Palmer, which is visible in the distance, its witches-hat turrets stretching skywards in marked contrast to the more reserved style of the château at Margaux. It is a regal château indeed, and certainly fitting in view of the quality of the wines that have been made here over the last couple of decades.

The history of Château Margaux stretches back to the 12th century, although this predates the construction of the building that we see today by about 700 years. It was not until the Lestonnac family took possession of the estate in the 16th century that it began to resemble the estate we know today, and by the beginning of the 18th century the estate at Margaux covered an impressive 265 hectares, of which one third was devoted to viticulture. The grand château was

added by the Marquis de la Colonilla, Bertrand Douat, in the early 19th century.

Ultimately Margaux fell on hard times, and found itself in the ownership of a committee of shareholders at the beginning of the 20th century. From here it passed to the Ginestet family, but under their tenure some very disappointing wines were produced during the 1960s and 1970s. The rescue came in the form of a Greek supermarket magnate, André Mentzelopoulos. He'd hardly had the tiller a year or two before he died, and his daughter Corrine inherited the property at a very tender age. Nevertheless, she is responsible for its renaissance, with the help of her right-hand man Paul Pontallier, who joined the team in 1983.

Today the estate is spread over 262 hectares, with 82 hectares of vines. The grape varieties are Cabernets Sauvignon (75%) and Franc (about 3%), Merlot (20%) and Petit Verdot (about 2%), whereas the white vineyards are planted solely with Sauvignon Blanc. What the team fashion here is a magnificent grand vin, which now sees a draconian selection with, in very recent vintages, only one-third of the harvest destined for this wine. Then there is a very worthwhile second wine, Pavillon Rouge du Château Margaux, as well as a recently introduced third wine. The white wine, Pavillon Blanc du Château Margaux, is also worth looking out for. All in all, these are truly excellent wines, which display fabulous elegance and a very harmonious depth.

At Château Margaux the wine is aged in barrels which are constructed on-site in the dedicated Margaux cooperage. This is situated next to the barrel cellars in the buildings that surround the château.

Château Haut-Brion

Best recent vintage: 2010 for red, 2008 for white
Also worth a look: 2005 for red, 2010 for white

The wine of Château Haut-Brion, particularly the red (although one should certainly not forget the white), has a character that seems unique and, even when placed alongside Pessac counterparts, seems to stand alone. It is not the superficial differences – most notably the unusual shape of the bottle – that matter; it is the savoury richness and complexity on the palate that sets it apart. This is great wine. The merchants that drew up the 1855 classification clearly thought so too; the wine was of adequate repute and commanded a sufficiently high price for it not only to be the sole Graves estate included in the 1855 classification of the Médoc, but for it to be ranked at the very highest level alongside Margaux, Lafite and Latour.

Its history is ancient, much more so than the more northerly estates of the Médoc. When St Julien and Pauillac were little more than boggy wastelands this estate was well established, the most notable of the early proprietors being Jean de Pontac, who owned Haut-Brion during the 16th century. Indeed, at this time it was known not as Château Haut-Brion, but as Château Pontac. Since then there have been many notable proprietors,

not least the French diplomat Talleyrand, but in modern times it has been the Dillon family, and through marriage the royal house of Luxembourg, that has controlled Haut-Brion. And they have done much to reinvigorate and restore the property, vineyards and wines to their former glory. Today Prince Robert of Luxembourg, ably assisted by technical director Jean-Bernard Delmas and then his son Jean-Philippe Delmas, continues the programme of improvements.

The vineyard is 45% Cabernet Sauvignon, 40% Merlot and 15% Cabernet Franc, as well as Sauvignon Blanc and Semillon for the white wines. The portfolio of wines is broad, because Pessac-Léognan allows for white and red wines. The grand vin is accompanied by a second wine, for many years called Bahans Haut-Brion but, from the 2007 vintage onwards, rechristened Clarence de Haut-Brion, in honour of Clarence Dillon. There is also the white Haut-Brion, a classic Bordeaux Semillon-Sauvignon Blanc blend which often vies for the position of top dry white wine in any Bordeaux vintage, as well as a second wine in this colour, La Clarté de Haut-Brion, which also takes fruit from the other principal Dillon-Luxembourg property, La Mission Haut-Brion.

I have come to adore these wines. They are visceral, earthy yet elegant, balanced and harmonious. They take what other properties of Pessac-Léognan offer and turn up the volume, offering greater intensity, depth and breadth of flavour. Yet they avoid caricature, remaining classically Graves, classically Bordeaux. They are wines which, if you have the financial clout, are absolutely worth ferreting away in the cellar.

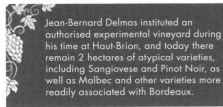

Jean-Bernard Delmas instituted an authorised experimental vineyard during his time at Haut-Brion, and today there remain 2 hectares of atypical varieties, including Sangiovese and Pinot Noir, as well as Malbec and other varieties more readily associated with Bordeaux.

Château d'Yquem

Best recent vintage: 2001
Also worth a look: 2009

When Eleanor of Aquitaine married Henri Plantagenet, who became King Henry II of England in 1154, Yquem came under British rule, and it remained so until the end of the Hundred Years War in 1453.

Château d'Yquem dominates the landscape of the Sauternes region. Situated near the peak at the centre of the southern half of the appellation it is visible for miles, and the rise offers a fine view of some of its near neighbours: Lafaurie Peyraguey, Rayne-Vigneau and Rieussec are just a few of the other châteaux surrounding the estate. It also dominates the 1855 classification of Sauternes and Barsac, sitting pretty in its own private ranking of premier cru supérieur, a step above the next ranking of quality. Unsurprisingly, it also dominates in terms of price; the wines of Château d'Yquem are several times more expensive than its neighbours. Of course, there is a quality distinction here as well; the wines produced here are some of the best sweet wines in the world.

The estate is truly ancient, dating back to the time of Eleanor of Aquitaine. It came into the hands of the Sauvage d'Yquem family in 1593, and they maintained ownership until the 18th century.

It then came to its most significant proprietors of recent times, the Lur-Saluces family, who continued here until control was gained, through the acquisition of a majority holding of shares from the various members of the Lur-Saluces family, by Bernard Arnault, head of the luxury goods group LVMH. In 2004 Alexandre Lur-Saluces was put out to pasture and Pierre Lurton, MD at Château Cheval Blanc (another LVMH property) took the reins. This remains the state of play today.

There are 100 hectares of vines in production at any one time, with a mix of 80% Semillon and 20% Sauvignon Blanc, with none of the permitted Muscadelle. The soils are variable, unsurprising for such a large estate, but there is much clay which necessitated the installation of field drains. The fruit is harvested in several passes through the vineyard as is the norm for Sauternes, and is destined for three separate cuvées. There is the grand vin, as well as what is by some considered to be the second wine, Château Haut-Charmes (although this is not officially acknowledged) as well as a distinctive dry wine, simply named Y.

The wines of Château d'Yquem do not impress with power or excess sweetness, rather these are wines that demonstrate a taut, linear concentration which is unparalleled. They offer something very distinctive within the appellation, Yquem's reputation rests not on a flashy style, but rather a fabulous elegance and poise. These are Sauternes that can dance across the palate when young, and in doing so display the structure that will enable long ageing in the cellar. Simply put, these are – in the best vintages – fabulous wines.

Château Cheval Blanc

LVMH investment has brought many benefits to Cheval Blanc, not least the construction of some new space age cellars, inaugurated during 2011.

Best recent vintage: 2008
Also worth a look: 2005

I s there any château more enigmatic than Cheval Blanc? This Premier Grand Cru Classé property (Class A, to set it and Ausone apart from the Class B hoi-polloi such as Canon, Pavie, and the like) occupies a unique position in St Emilion and Bordeaux. With its mysterious name, vineyards dominated by Cabernet Franc and, cutting to the chase, a history of turning out simply fabulous wines, it's no wonder Cheval Blanc is an irresistible lure for so many. And I include myself in this group of people who find themselves readily drawn to Cheval Blanc.

Although the origins of the name, Cheval Blanc, are difficult to elucidate, the history behind more tangible components of the estate are not so reticent. It was in 1832 that the first part of what was to become Cheval Blanc was acquired by the Ducasse family, an offshoot of the Figeac estate.

The wine was originally sold under the Figeac label, it being made many years before the owners, the Laussac-Fourcaud family, began to market it as Cheval Blanc. During the early 20th century it was Albert Fourcaud-Laussac (for some reason he reversed his surname) who ran the show, and his descendents continued on at the estate until, like Yquem, the property was bought by luxury goods group LVMH, working with Belgian businessman Albert Frère. They installed Pierre Lurton as estate manager; Lurton now divides his time between Cheval Blanc and his other chief property, Yquem.

The vineyard is 57% Cabernet Franc, with the balance mostly Merlot augmented by a little Cabernet Sauvignon and Malbec, and the property is situated right on the border with the Pomerol appellation; standing on the steps of the château gives a wonderful view of Pomerol, and a number of famous wine estates. The grand vin is joined by a second wine, Le Petit Cheval. The former is often a blend of not-quite equal proportions, typically dominated by Cabernet Franc (although 2009 was an exception with only 40%) and the balance is Merlot, whereas Le Petit Cheval sees more variation, with a Cabernet Franc component that has ranged in recent vintages from 25% to 70%. The grand vin is frequently regarded as the wine world's greatest expression of Cabernet Franc, conveniently overlooking the fact that Merlot makes up a significant proportion in most vintages. Whether or not this is true, there is no doubt in my mind that this is a great wine. And the second wine, sold for much less, frequently performs very well.

Château Ausone

Best recent vintage: 2009
Also worth a look: 2008

This estate is, quite rightly I think, considered by many to be St Emilion's preeminent vineyard. I shall never forget my first visit to Ausone; it sits at the end of a steep ascent along a narrow and rather winding track, just wide enough for one vehicle to pass. On arrival I wondered where the vines might be; many are over the wall to one side, closer to St Emilion itself, but in a slightly surreal fashion the closest were those growing five metres or more above me, crowning the stone doorway to Ausone's barrel cellar. This gives the slight feel of claustrophobia, of everything being crammed into too tight a space. Ausone is not an estate with the spacious facilities of the left bank first growths; there are no green courtyards dotted with plane trees as at Latour, and no richly coloured reception rooms, dotted with portraiture as at Lafite. Nevertheless, this is undoubtedly one of the leading Bordeaux estates of the 21st century, and this success is largely down to Alain Vauthier, Ausone's proprietor.

The estate came to Vauthier not by the smoothest of routes. During the early years of the 20th century the property was in the ownership of the Dubois-Challon family. Cécile Dubois-Challon married into the Vauthier family, and

they were blessed with children and then grandchildren. Jean Dubois-Challon married but had no children, nevertheless after his death his widow was determined to hold onto what she regarded as her share of the vineyard. Acrimony between the two branches of the family meant that management of their estates (they owned more than just Ausone) was difficult, and some aspects of the long-running dispute saw the two sides face each other in court, often fighting over minor details. Eventually Jean's widow Heylette Dubois-Challon tired of her situation and she resolved to sell Ausone which, after some legal wrangling, was acquired by none other than Alain Vauthier, Cécile's grandson. Heylette Dubois-Challon, meanwhile, won the right to live on in the château, which she did until her death in 2003.

Now in full control of Château Ausone, Alain Vauthier, joined more recently by his daughter Pauline, has been improving the estate and wine. There's no doubt that they have succeeded in pushing the quality to the point where the château sits, in my opinion, right at the top of the St Emilion commune. They have increased the focus on Cabernet Franc rather than Merlot. There are a mere 7 hectares of vines, mostly positioned in a sun trap, an amphitheatre of vines protected from frost, below the property. There are also a few vines, as I alluded above, up above the barrel cellar. The resulting wine is extraordinarily expensive, but is also of exceptional elegance and style, making this one of the most desirable addresses in all Bordeaux. For those with a more limited financial reach the estate's second wine, Chapelle d'Ausone, is certainly worth considering.

The Vauthiers also produce a range of wines from neighbouring St Emilion estates, including Fonbel, Moulin-Saint-Georges, Simard and Haut-Simard. These are well worth buying and drinking.

Petrus

Best recent vintage: 2010
Also worth a look: 2005

I s the Petrus of today the most famous estate in Bordeaux? If so it would hardly be surprising; Petrus is one of a trio of right bank wines – the others being Le Pin and Ausone – which now sell at astronomical prices, typically thousands of pounds, dollars or euros per case (if not per bottle), and when you're so expensive you're also going to be highly newsworthy. I suspect such widespread knowledge of the wine is largely vicarious; in the case of Petrus I imagine it is more often than not based on occasional tabloid reports of expensive dinners at Michelin-starred restaurants where traders and bankers blow their recently acquired bonuses in the most conspicuous fashion possible. Such dinners frequently seem to include Petrus, usually squeezed between the vintage Krug and Yquem, proving that this particular Pomerol has, in circles devoted to conspicuous consumption at least, become something of an icon.

And yet in the mid-20th century, just a few decades ago, Petrus was a little known estate in an appellation regarded as a minor satellite of St Emilion; the wines were sometimes difficult to sell, and the prices were low. It has been a meteoric rise to stardom under the tenure first of Madame Edmond Loubat, and then the Moueix family, for this modern-day prince of Pomerol.

The Moueix family are a local dynasty who today own or administer many of the top estates of Pomerol, not just Petrus. Other properties include Château Trotanoy and Lafleur-Gazin as well as half a dozen others.

But this is very recent history, and the Petrus story begins at least a century earlier. It was during the early 20th century, particularly between the two World Wars, that Petrus broke away from the rest of the Pomerol pack. The property came into the ownership of Madame Edmond Loubat whose passion for her domaine was legendary. Many of her business dealings were managed by the Moueix family, and Petrus itself is today theirs, having been acquired in a slightly piecemeal fashion from the Loubat family.

Much of the ethereal quality of Petrus is put down to the vineyard, which is notable for the Petrus boutonnière (or Petrus button), a mound 40 metres above sea level comprising a rich blue clay, the surrounding soils more gravelly although still clay-rich. Beneath there is a thick seam of iron-rich subsoil known as crasse de fer which characterises the Pomerol vineyards. It is the blue clay that makes Petrus unique; although it extends over some of the neighbouring properties, at Petrus this clay covers pretty much the entire vineyard. Merlot is suited to clay of course, and the vineyard here is almost entirely given over to this variety. The wine that comes from this vineyard, which for years was made by Jean-Claude Berrouet, is today – since the 2008 vintage – made by his son, Olivier Berrouet. The wines are, put simply, sublime. There is a reason, after all, for the eye-watering price tag.

Le Pin

Best recent vintage: 2008
Also worth a look: 2006

The meteoric rise to stardom of Le Pin has been incredible. A few decades ago this was an unknown estate. Thanks to its current proprietors the vineyard has been lifted from anonymity to take its place, in my opinion, alongside the top first growths of the region.

The story begins in 1924 with the acquisition of the vineyard by a Madame Laubie. It was not yet Le Pin as we know it; the wines were sold as generic Pomerol, and this remained the situation until the elderly lady's death in 1979. During her time there was little income and no investment, which goes some way to explaining the state of the rather tumbledown house at Le Pin (which has recently been demolished and replaced with new cellars in 2011). It may also have contributed, in part at least, to the current quality of the wines; with no money or chemical treatments in the vineyard the soils were pure and unsullied, the vines healthy. With her passing, the property, with a little over one hectare of vines, was acquired by the Thienpont family. There has only been one minor change since, with the addition of a small plot of adjacent vines, purchased by Jacques Thienpont. From the outset the wine was reputedly of very good quality, but being a backwater Pomerol, was something of an insider's wine. It sold well, although not at an exorbitant price. Le Pin is something of an accidental superstar, and it is only with the passage of time, thanks to excellent quality

The Thienpont family have had great success in the Pomerol appellation. Jacques' cousin, Alexandre, is proprietor of nearby Vieux Château Certan.

combined with scarcity, and comparisons with first growths, such as Petrus and the like, that the price has really rocketed towards the stratosphere.

The vines include 8% Cabernet Franc but are otherwise all Merlot, and the wine itself is 100% Merlot. Once harvested by hand, the wine is fermented in stainless steel vats before going into barrel. Two vintages will generally occupy no more than 70 barrels, such is the small scale of production here. Only 500-700 cases are produced each year.

Le Pin, most people report, was named for the solitary pine tree that stands adjacent to the property. I find this rather difficult to reconcile with the sight of at least two such pine trees outside the house, which suggests to me that Les Pins would have been more appropriate (I've since been told that the second was planted in case the first blew down). Nevertheless, Le Pin it was named, and the first vintage bottled by the Thienpont family was labelled so back in 1979. Sadly whereas I have not tasted every vintage back to that inaugural year, what I have had the pleasure of tasting suggests to me that this is one of the greatest Bordeaux wines in existence.

GRAND VIN

CHATEAU
...H... BAGES
...ND CRU CLASSÉ
...PAUILLAC
...TION PAUILLAC CONTROLEE

...iétaire à PAUILLAC (FRANCE).
...PRODUCE OF FRANCE
13.0% VOL.

750ml

5

Top 20 Châteaux

This subjective and personal list serves to highlight 20 of what I consider to be the most interesting châteaux, turning out the most exciting wines in Bordeaux today. These are the movers and shakers, châteaux producing the most dynamic, forthright wines, often reflecting the drive, ambition and personality of their proprietors. In nearly all cases the people concerned are responsible for the dramatic revitalisation of these once under-performing wine estates.

Château Pontet-Canet

Best recent vintage: **2009**
Also worth a look: **1996**

I doubt there is any poster-child for the winds of change that have swept through Bordeaux in recent years (specifically towards the end of the 20th century and the beginning of the 21st) quite like Pontet-Canet. A lowly cinquième cru, (despite its proximity to the more exalted estates of Pauillac, including both Lafite and Mouton), this once-derided estate was reduced – during the mid-20th century – to nothing more than a brand name for a lowly non-vintage table wine served on the French railways. If the first growths were aristocrats enjoying cocktails and canapés up front, Pontet-Canet was the poor relative, huddled in third class with the Great Unwashed. I think it's fair to say that Pontet-Canet has known such destitution, but those times have passed and the winds of change mentioned above have blown strong at the estate. The bringer of this change was Guy Tesseron, his son Alfred and, more recently, his granddaughter Melanie.

Under the direction of the Tesserons, together with winemaker Jean-Michel Comme, this is now one of the leading estates in Bordeaux. The revolution began in the 1990s, with the introduction of green-harvesting. This brave new direction initially caused a rift between Alfred and his father, but when the quality of the finished wine proved so obviously superior to what had been produced before, Guy ceded full control to Alfred. Since then the changes have been huge, including the reintroduction of horses – last seen in the Pontet-Canet vineyard in 1959 – and the conversion of the vineyards to biodynamic viticulture, this being the only classed growth château to have taken such a direction. The winemaking facilities have also been overhauled with the introduction of new egg-shaped vats, as well as new wooden vessels.

During the 1990s there was a change in quality without overt change in style at Pontet-Canet, the wines showing balance and style with moderate substance and texture. From 2000 onwards, however, not only has quality continued to rise but the style has evolved in tandem, no doubt heavily influenced by the Tesseron-Comme innovations at the property. Ultimately the wines are deeper, more concentrated and more substantial. In their youth they seem burlier and are loaded with tannin, colour and extract, yet still possess an original sense of balance, in that all the Pontet-Canet components are present and correct. There's no doubting the wines have come a long way since the mid-1990s. They have a richer, more textured feel too, bolstered by a style of fruit less traditional than it once was, having now a more creamed-confit-forest-fruit character. Nevertheless, these are brave, modern wines in the best possible mold, and have – quite rightly – garnered a lot of praise.

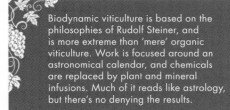

Biodynamic viticulture is based on the philosophies of Rudolf Steiner, and is more extreme than 'mere' organic viticulture. Work is focused around an astronomical calendar, and chemicals are replaced by plant and mineral infusions. Much of it reads like astrology, but there's no denying the results.

Château Lynch-Bages

Best recent vintage: 2010
Also worth a look: 2005

L ike Pontet-Canet, Château Lynch-Bages is also classified as a fifth growth, and is another property which further illustrates the single most important failing of the 1855 classification. This is that although some aspects of the classification remain applicable today, many are outdated, and the track record of over-performance exhibited by Lynch-Bages is as good an example of this as any.

As well as the red, Lynch-Bages is one of the few left-bank Bordeaux châteaux that also produces a white wine. The Blanc de Lynch-Bages is part-fermented in new oak barrels with six months on its lees (dead yeast sediment) before bottling.

When I first started learning about Bordeaux, Lynch-Bages was a real insiders' wine; those with more experienced palates than my own would rave about Lynch-Bages, or "Lunch-Bags" as it was affectionately known. These happy Bordeaux savants knew a good wine when they tasted it, and had long recognised that under the tenure of the Cazes family this cinquième cru was turning out wines more befitting of a deuxième. Indeed, some wine writers that I read at the time clearly regarded some older vintages as capable of challenging the first growths when tasted in comparison. Lynch-Bages was, for many, a 'must-buy' wine in any vintage.

The modern era for Lynch-Bages begins with its purchase by Jean-Charles Cazes in 1939. At first a baker and then a banker, the multi-talented Cazes moved in at Lynch-Bages as a tenant, quickly taking on the responsibility of making

the wine. Five years later he purchased the estate from his landlord, and set about rescuing the dilapidated château and neglected vineyards, some of which had been used for growing potatoes in favour of vines. His industry laid the foundation for the success Lynch-Bages enjoys today, and the good work has been continued by his descendents. Control first passed to Jean-Charles' son André, then to his incomparable grandson Jean-Michel, and most recently to his great grandson, Jean-Charles.

Although my tasting colleagues of old faithfully put their money into every vintage of "Lunch-Bags", my tastings of more recent vintages might instigate a rethink. I recognised that while quality here was very high, the ultra-reliability had faded a little. Yes, there were good wines here, wines that would stand up well in a comparative tasting with other Pauillac estates ranked as fifth growths, but in my opinion they were not comparable with the two Pichons, which were performing very well. Nevertheless, in the most recent of vintages I have seen more polish and power from Lynch-Bages than before, and particular successes – in admittedly favourable vintages such as 2009 and 2010 – have forced me to accept there is certainly something very special here. It doesn't show in every vintage, but when the Cazes family get it right, these wines clearly have the potential to blow a portion of the competition away. I hope that under the tenure of Jean-Charles, the latest Cazes, this high level of quality will be maintained.

Château Léoville-Barton

Best recent vintage: 2010
Also worth a look: 2005

The wines of Anthony Barton, and most specifically those of Château Léoville-Barton, exist in a unique place, and there are few wines held in such high regard by the press, trade and consumer that manage to offer such good value for money. Add in an amiable proprietor, of Irish descent, who has been outspoken on the matter of Bordeaux as a drink for giving pleasure, rather than an investment vehicle, and you have something close to the perfect Bordeaux château.

The history of the Barton family in this region can be traced back to 1722, when Irishman Thomas Barton left his native Curraghmore for foreign shores, settling in Bordeaux. Here he established a wine trading company, this region being a natural choice for such a venture thanks to the ready supply of fine wines and a major Atlantic seaport for export. His descendent Hugh Barton purchased part of the Léoville estate, which was broken up and sold off after the French Revolution. Hence Léoville-Barton was born, and passed down to its current proprietor, the aforementioned Anthony.

Until recent vintages, Léoville-Barton has had a place in the hearts of many claret drinkers

thanks to a winning combination of good quality – the property is frequently referred to as one of Bordeaux's super-seconds – and great value. Anthony Barton was the claret drinker's dream proprietor – turning out fabulous wines sold at fair prices. In great vintages, such as 2000, Château Léoville-Barton would often have a prix de sortie several hundred pounds less than comparable wines from other highly regarded second growth estates. This practice was wholly admirable, and I applaud Anthony Barton for maintaining his philosophy that wine should be drunk, and not seen as a trading opportunity. Sadly, however, there were downsides. These included (unsubstantiated) rumours that this philosophy was unpopular with neighbouring proprietors, who appeared avaricious when their prices were contrasted with Monsieur Barton's.

Anthony also lost out financially. Brisk trading saw asking prices for some vintages of Léoville-Barton double within days of their release; naturally, none of that money ever found its way back to the château, but merely lined the pockets of traders and wheeler-dealers. As a result initial prices have risen over the last decade, and in the most desirable of recent vintages, namely 2005, 2009 and 2010, prices here have been comparable to other estates. Happily, this is combined with extraordinarily high quality.

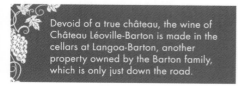

Devoid of a true château, the wine of Château Léoville-Barton is made in the cellars at Langoa-Barton, another property owned by the Barton family, which is only just down the road.

Château Pichon-Lalande

Best recent vintage: **2010**
Also worth a look: **2009**

T he early history of Château Pichon-Lalande naturally matches that of its twin sibling, Pichon-Baron, the two having both been created from the great Pichon estate. One part of the estate came to an heiress named Marie-Laure, who had married Comte Henri de Lalande in 1818, and thus the estate became known as Château Pichon-Comtesse de Lalande (or Pichon-Lalande, for short). That the property was initially passed down the female side of the family seems somehow appropriate in modern times, and at the end of the 20th century the estate had another strong woman at the helm, May-Eliane de Lencquesaing, who had inherited a portion of it from her father, Edouard Miailhe, a famous name in Bordeaux.

Having proceeded to acquire a majority stake in the property, May-Eliane began a programme of development at the château, starting with bringing in new staff to manage the estate and make the wine. The cellars were extended and re-equipped, before entirely new facilities were added in 1986. That they could make these changes was down to May-Eliane's majority ownership, and her position of authority was maintained until very recently. In the decades that have passed since May-Eliane assumed control, the quality of the produce has rocketed, and these wines are testament to the time and effort this imposing lady has invested in the estate.

Nevertheless time waits for no man (or woman) and with her advancing age, and the lack of an obvious heir, it was perhaps natural that Madame de Lencquesaing should look for outside investment in Pichon-Lalande. In a surprise announcement in 2007 it was revealed that Pichon-Lalande had been acquired by none other than the Rouzaud family of Champagne Roederer. It was all-change again, with the appointment by the Rouzaud family of Sylvie Cazes – younger sister to Jean-Michel Cazes of Château Lynch-Bages – as director of the estate. Thankfully so far, the wines produced under Sylvie's leadership look to be every bit as good as they were under her illustrious predecessor.

Now, I wouldn't say that I have acquaintances willing to sell a kidney for a case of Pichon-Lalande (although sometimes I have wondered whether I might), but certainly I have met many who hold the wines of this particular Pichon in very high regard. For the last few decades the wines have been some of the most consistent in Bordeaux, with only the occasional blip – although admittedly these blips seem to have occurred in perfectly good vintages (1990 and 2005, for example), when one might have expected better from the château. Equally, however, there are lesser vintages when the team at Pichon-Lalande has turned out excellent wines against all odds, with the 1991 being a prime example. Certainly the wines are distinctive, sometimes exotic, and very frequently of a high quality.

Château Pichon-Baron

Best recent vintage: 2009
Also worth a look: 2000

I f you are in search of a true fairy tale château, you could do worse than go to Bordeaux. There are several contenders, but perhaps one of the strongest is Château Pichon-Baron (or Château Longueville au Baron de Pichon-Longueville – to give its full title). The keen, conical roofs sitting atop their circular towers lend the building a magical feel. Its reflection (shimmering in the recently constructed pool, beneath which hide the underground cellars and winemaking facilities) does nothing to distract from its natural beauty and grandeur.

As with Château Pichon-Lalande, the seeds of Château Pichon-Baron's creation lie in the break-up of the original Pichon estate. Here the property was passed down the male line, to Raoul, who assumed the title of Baron. It continued down the same line until 1933, by which time the family seems to have run out of heirs, and the estate was sold. By the 1970s and 1980s it was clear that the wines made at Château Pichon-Baron lacked the quality expected of such a highly ranked property. This was the state of affairs when Jean-Michel Cazes (of Château Lynch-Bages) and AXA Millésimes (an esoteric "viticultural investment" string in the bow of the insurance company AXA) became involved. The new owners had huge capacity for investment, so it came as no surprise that Pichon-Baron quickly experienced a serious amount of change. The result of new investment was a heady rise in quality, and under Jean-Michel Cazes the wines of Pichon-Baron

soon began to challenge – and not infrequently usurp – those of Pichon Lalande. Previously, in my opinion, there had been no competition.

Today, Pichon-Baron is managed by Christian Seely, Jean-Michel Cazes having retired from his role in 2000. By this time the reputation of Pichon-Baron had been restored, with a string of admirable wines produced during the latter years of the preceding decade. A newly equipped chai and bottling line were completed in 1991, while new practices were implemented in the cellar...yet the improvements weren't to stop there. It was to my disappointment that, on espying the château in late 2006, it bore a greater resemblance to a building site than a fairy tale castle. But the house itself was untouched, the work concerning the cellars beneath the pool in front of the château. More work, more improvements, more investment, and happily today the site has returned to its pristine glory. Meanwhile Seely pushes the wine quality even further. Stricter selection has been key to this, Seely looking to the historic heart of the estate, a central 40 hectares, as his source for the grand vin. He has also introduced smaller fermentation vats, enabling plot-by-plot vinifications. With continued commitment like this, we should see more great wines from Pichon-Baron in the not to distant future, I am sure.

AXA Millésimes own an impressive portfolio of properties in Bordeaux, including Suduiraut, Petit Village and Pibran (alongside Pichon-Baron). All are managed by Christian Seely and quality is high across the board, especially here and at Suduiraut.

Château Léoville-Las-Cases

Best recent vintage: 2010
Also worth a look: 2005

T he story of Léoville-Las-Cases looms out of the marshland that predates the planting of vines on the Médoc peninsula, although for our purposes things only start getting interesting when the original Léoville estate – precursor of today's Léoville trio – is split up. The heart of the original estate found its way into Léoville-Las-Cases, and at that time the property remained in the hands of the Las-Cases family, although Théophile Skawinski, the general manager, was sold a portion of land. He passed his share onto André Delon, who proceeded to acquire a greater and greater portion of the shares in Las-Cases, until his family eventually became the majority shareholders. Today great grandson Jean-Hubert is in control and has around 100 hectares at his disposal, of which half is in a single block to the north of the

château, whilst a significant portion, about 20 hectares, lies further inland, and is used in the production of a parallel wine which is named Clos du Marquis.

In the Léoville order, Las-Cases is the most impressive of the three estates (the pre-eminent estate in all St Julien, nonetheless). It is the first and most tangible challenger to the first growths and the prime example of a 'super-second', those pretenders to the premier cru crown. As recently as 2008, a Cornell University study suggested that it should be promoted to first growth status (alongside a demotion for Mouton), an opinion based on ratings of the wine over 35 vintages, from 1970 to 2005. The estate is made up of the original Léoville lands, it being the larger part while portions were carved off in the creation of the Barton and Poyferré vineyards. And whereas the latter two estates have been owned by a number of different families, Las-Cases remained, for a long time, in the ownership of the descendents of the Marquis de Las-Cases. Even throughout the 20th century they retained a minority share, long after control was ceded to the Delon family.

If the history and pedigree of the property doesn't impress, one has simply to taste the wines. Encountering a Barton or a Poyferré is a fine experience; these are, after all, great wines, and in recent vintages the estates seem to have taken quality to the next level, especially Poyferré. But Las-Cases, in my experience, is more likely to stop a taster in their tracks. Other châteaux may obtain these dizzy heights from time to time; I can think of one or two vintages of Léoville-Barton and Gruaud-Larose that touch first growth status, but Las-Cases has the character to do so with splendid regularity. Even in lesser vintages, the wines remain sublime, or at least better than the competition. The prime example in recent years is the 2008, which stunned me during the primeur tastings in April 2009; what a brilliant effort from an outstanding estate.

Château Montrose

Best recent vintage: 2010
Also worth a look: 1995

I n researching the history of Bordeaux vineyards I regularly find myself delving into medieval history, finding stories of 12th-century fortresses, ancient seigneuries and the Hundred Years' War. Not so with Château Montrose, which is one of the youngest classed growths in the Médoc. At the end of the 18th century the land which today is the Montrose vineyard was nothing more than heather-encrusted moorland, owned by the Ségur family. It was Etienne Théodore Dumoulin who cleared the heather and scrub, and found the soil beneath eminently suitable for the vine. Planting was underway by 1815 with good results, and by 1820 Dumoulin had expanded the vineyard and erected a small château. Fast work indeed!

The estate subsequently came to the enlightened Mathieu Dollfus, who not only extended the cellars and constructed new accommodation for the workers, but also introduced profit sharing and health care for his employees, both radical practices for the 19th century. It wasn't long before Montrose was more a village than a wine estate, complete with its own railway to transport the wines from the cellars down to the river, before being shipped upstream to Bordeaux.

Eventually the property came into the hands of the Charmolüe family, who held onto the estate until it was acquired by construction and telecommunications magnates the Bouygues brothers, Martin and Olivier. They took control of a large vineyard, 67 hectares in all, but under their tenure it has seen considerable expansion, with new purchases swelling it to 95 hectares. Much of this increase in surface area is accounted for by the purchase in 2010 of 22 hectares (of which 21.5 were planted with vines) from Thierry Gardinier of Phélan-Ségur, which lies just to the north of Montrose. The other really significant change here was the installation of Jean-Bernard Delmas, onetime winemaker at Haut-Brion, in charge of the cellars. He presided over the primeur tastings at Montrose, showing not only the wines of the Montrose estate but also those of the Bouygues brothers' other acquisition, Tronquoy-Lalande. Whereas Montrose offers the grandeur, Tronquoy-Lalande offers the value. The 2011 vintage was Delmas' last, however, as retirement now beckons, but Hervé Berland – recently of Mouton-Rothschild – has been appointed his replacement.

Montrose is a property that offers great consistency through most vintages, and also has a propensity to age very well, with bottles showing excellently after many decades in the cellar.

Château Léoville-Poyferré

Best recent vintage: 2009
Also worth a look: 2008

As with Léoville-Barton and Léoville-Las-Cases, Léoville-Poyferré has its origins in the grand Léoville estate that dominated St Julien in the 17th and 18th centuries. This portion came, after having been sold off, to a daughter of the Las-Cases family who then married Baron Jean-Marie de Poyferré, and thus the vineyards became Léoville-Poyferré. It was not in the ownership of the family for a very long time, mere decades in fact, nevertheless the name has stuck through to modern times. Much more significant in the history of this estate are the Cuvelier family, who acquired the land in the late-19th century...and who still own it today.

The acquisition of Léoville-Poyferré was without doubt the jewel in the Cuvelier crown. Nevertheless they did not choose to direct the operations of their new acquisition themselves, instead electing to install a manager. Originally the arrangement worked well, and quality at Léoville-Poyferré was high, but over the ensuing decades the situation deteriorated, and the caliber of the wine slipped. Quality hit rock bottom during the 1960s and 1970s but, as they say, the night is darkest before the dawn, and in 1979 the baton was passed to Max's son, Didier Cuvelier. The fact that Didier was a trained accountant might not have inspired much hope of salvation, but his arrival in fact marked the beginning of the Poyferré renaissance, which has continued into the early years of the 21st century.

Under Didier there was extensive investment, particularly in the vineyard, with increased planting of Cabernet Sauvignon being one

important change. There was extensive modernisation of the facilities too: the cellars were rebuilt in 1984 and then again in 1990, underground water storage was installed in 1983, and a tasting room was added – as was plenty of new wood in the cellars (recent vintages have seen as much as 75% new oak). With Didier Cuvelier at the helm, things at Léoville-Poyferré were looking up. There were a number of favourable vintages during the 1980s, particularly 1982, 1983 and 1985, and the estate produced some lovely wines in this period. During the 1990s and early years of the 21st century, quality has really been in the ascendant, and it seems that Poyferré is once again fulfilling its potential, regularly producing the standard of wines for which it was once renowned. Léoville-Poyferré is no longer the black sheep of the Léoville family; this estate now plays on an equal footing with Léoville-Barton, and indeed in some vintages may produce the superior wine. They have different styles, of course, Barton being the more reserved, harder, traditional style (in contrast to Poyferré's slightly more voluptuous nature) but there is little difference between them in terms of absolute quality.

Château Ducru-Beaucaillou

During the 19th century the vineyards of Bordeaux were plagued by mildew. The discovery of the cure – copper sulphate, which until then had been used solely to deter thieves from stealing the fruit (which it coloured blue) – was made at Ducru-Beaucaillou.

Best recent vintage: 2009
Also worth a look: 1995

19

What is it about Ducru-Beaucaillou that seems to captivate some Bordeaux acolytes, and yet alienate others? I know some who consider it their desert-island claret, who wax lyrical about their favourite bottles, and hoard them in anticipation of special meals and evenings, for moments free of disruption and distraction when they can lose themselves in the wine. I also know some who find the wine utterly unappealing, and wish themselves not so much free of distractions, but free of Ducru altogether! It certainly has an elegant style, perhaps accentuated over the last couple of decades, that demands attention. One man's elegant is another's lack of substance, I suppose. My own encounters with the estate have, however, been largely positive, even if they haven't been as regular as I would like.

The origin of the Ducru-Beaucaillou vineyards may be traced back to the 17th century, when they were once part of a much larger property, Beychevelle. The seeds that grew into Ducru-Beaucaillou and also Branaire-Ducru were sown in 1642 when, following the death of Beychevelle's proprietor Bernard de Valette, otherwise known as the Duc d'Epernon, the property was sold off in order to settle his not inconsiderable debts. Thereafter the estate passed through many pairs of hands, most notably Nathaniel Johnston in the 19th century who was responsible for an extensive refurbishment of the château (including the addition of a tower at either end of the building, giving it the distinctive appearance we know today).

In modern times it is the Borie family who hold court here, Bruno Borie taking control from brother François-Xavier – who left to focus on the family's other estate, Grand-Puy-Lacoste – in 2003. It was the Borie family that really boosted the fortunes of Ducru-Beaucaillou, with 1995 considered the turning point, a fantastic vintage, and the wines have been excellent ever since. Recent vintages have seen new benchmarks for the estate in terms of quality, I suspect longevity also, and most certainly pricing, the 2009 being the most expensive release of Ducru-Beaucaillou ever. A prodigious effort, infused with tannins piled upon tannins, this is a wine which will be enjoyed by our grandchildren, and perhaps also by the more long-lived among us. If I were to survive on my desert island long enough to see the wine mature, I am sure Ducru would make my list.

Château Cos d'Estournel

Best recent vintage: 2005
Also worth a look: 2004

I t was late on a December afternoon when I first saw Cos d'Estournel; it was the week before Christmas, and I was in the region for a few days of tasting. Within the car it was warm, but outside the mercury was falling fast and above the sky darkened as night advanced. And there, situated on a turn in the road just ahead, catching a few final, fading rays, brooded the Oriental pagodas and golden sandstone of the magnificent cellars at Cos d'Estournel.

The exotic appearance of Cos d'Estournel's fabulous château is down to Louis Gaspard d'Estournel, a 19th-century proprietor who when renovating his buildings eschewed the usual materials in favour of the aforementioned sandstone. In terms of design the château is also a departure from the regional norm, no doubt taking inspiration from his many travels in the Orient and the East, travels which had brought him the nickname the Maharajah of St Estèphe. The cellars sprouted tall pagodas which would look more at home than in a Chinese temple than in the Médoc. The doorway, decorated with vines, grapes, flowers and leaves, was imported from the Palace of Zanzibar. And against the road he

constructed an imposing triumphal arch, rather like the one found at Léoville-Las-Cases.

One cannot help but feel, on reviewing Louis Gaspard's story, that he was something of a showman, and I think the same might be true of Cos d'Estournel's modern-day administrator, Jean-Guillaume Prats. Having said that, there's no doubting Jean-Guillaume is also an extremely shrewd businessman, and his hard work and commitment to Cos d'Estournel over the years has ensured it remains one of the top estates in Bordeaux. But there is flair here too, and recent renovations to the property have been both sympathetic and innovative, with no expense spared. Architecturally the restoration work is admirable, but it is the sheer scale of the project which, should you be lucky enough to visit the estate, will take your breath away.

Jean-Guillaume has not steered totally clear of controversy, his wines being somewhat divisive. Back in the 1990s the wines were elegant, firm and composed, whereas now they are powerhouse wines that display more concentration and tannin than many thought possible. The 2009 was a case in point; tasting at the estate in early 2010, I found it a huge and overbearingly tannic wine, clearly of high quality and the product of great investment and effort, but missing the finesse and gentle aristocratic grace it once possessed. Happily, things were reined in somewhat in 2010, enough to satisfy many, although those questioning the estate's direction still remain (including, I must admit, myself). Nevertheless, the always intriguing Cos d'Estournel certainly deserves its place in the Bordeaux Top 20 this year.

There is a little known curiosity at Cos d'Estournel, a limited-production white wine with a (high) price tag to match that of the red wine. A blend of Sauvignon Blanc and Semillon, controversially the wine is not sourced from vineyards contiguous with those of Cos d'Estournel.

Château Trotanoy

Best recent vintage: **2010**
Also worth a look: **2008**

Trotanoy is one of the more venerable estates of Pomerol, dating back to when viticulture was first established in the region. At the time it was in the ownership of the Giraud family, royal courtiers from nearby Libourne, and it was most probably they who were the first to plant vines on the estate. It was they who began the shift from arable polyculture towards a situation in which the vine would dominate the landscape absolutely, as it does in Pomerol today.

At this time the Giraud land was referred to as Trop-Ennuie, as evidenced by documents from the late 18th century. This literally translates into "too annoying", and it is commonly said the name refers to the Trotanoy soils which, being a mix of thick clay and gravel, are tiresome to work, either by hand or plough. Nevertheless the work must have paid some dividends because during the 19th century the estate was comfortably positioned with the best of the appellation, including Vieux Château Certan and La Conseillante. It is safe to say it is still held in high regard by anybody who knows the wines of this appellation well.

Ultimately the Girauds sold to the Pecresse

Établissements Jean-Pierre Moueix is a firm headed up by father-and-son team Christian and Edouard Moueix. It owns or manages many of the top estates in Pomerol, including not only Petrus and Trotanoy, but also Providence, Latour à Pomerol, Lafleur-Gazin and Hosanna. The company also manages a number of estates in neighbouring St Emilion.

family who, in 1953, sold the estate to its current proprietors: the Moueix family of Libourne. It was Jean-Pierre Moueix that struck the deal, and today the property is administered, managed and marketed by the next two generations of this right bank dynasty, Christian and Edouard Moueix, as well as Christian's cousin Jean-Jacques Moueix, who resides at the property. Moueix is a very famous family in this part of Bordeaux, owning and/or managing as they do a large number of very significant estates around Pomerol, including the mighty Petrus. They have just 7.5 hectares of vines planted at Trotanoy on soils of gravel and sand over the deeper crasse de fer, the rock-hard layer of iron-rich soil that lies beneath many of these Libournais vineyards.

For many years at the annual Bordeaux primeur tasting each April, Trotanoy has been shown alongside Petrus at the Moueix quayside offices, perhaps to its disadvantage. Petrus has the capability to overshadow just about any wine, including Trotanoy. In more recent years, however, Petrus has been removed from the tasting (visitors to the region must visit Petrus itself if they wish to taste the wine) allowing Trotanoy – now top of the tree – to really shine. If it was not clear before what fabulous quality can be found here, it certainly should be now!

APPELLATION POMEROL CONTRÔLÉE

CHÂTEAU TROTANOY

POMEROL

2009

SOCIÉTÉ CIVILE DU CHÂTEAU TROTANOY
PROPRIÉTAIRE A POMEROL (GIRONDE)

Château Grand-Puy-Lacoste

Best recent vintage: 2010
Also worth a look: 2008

The lowest rung of the 1855 classification, the cinquièmes crus, is dominated by the châteaux of Pauillac, which take up 12 of the 18 slots. A number of this Bordeaux dozen seriously under-perform on a regular basis, but the rest provide us with a spectrum of quality ranging from good to superb. Many of these estates – especially those that neighbour the Pauillac firsts of Latour, Lafite and Mouton – comfortably exceed their own classification, and behave more like super-seconds. Lynch-Bages is an old favourite for many (including myself), frequently paraded as an example of an over-performing estate, even if concerns of fluctuating quality levels are occasionally raised. And for many today it is surely the revitalised, turbo-charged Pontet-Canet that springs to mind as offering the greatest quality among the cinquièmes crus. But let us not overlook Grand-Puy-Lacoste; an estate that regularly produces superb wines.

The origins of Grand-Puy-Lacoste lie in an estate that existed in the northern parts of the commune in the Middle Ages. The estate sits on the Grand Puy, one of the many gravel hills along the Médoc, and boasts soils perfect for Cabernet Sauvignon, a vine associated with many of the greatest vineyards of the region. Neighbouring Grand-Puy-Ducasse, an estate producing a wine less desirable than that of Grand-Puy-Lacoste, also has its origins in this ancient domaine.

In the mid-20th century the estate was in the hands of Raymond Dupin, an absentee landlord, and perhaps as a consequence the estate fell into decline. It was only with the arrival of the Borie family – first Jean-Eugène and more recently François-Xavier Borie, who moved from Ducru-Beaucaillou (leaving the running of that estate to his younger brother, Bruno) – that things started to improve. Under François-Xavier there has been an impressive programme of investment and innovation. This began in the vineyard and spread to the cellars, with increased attention to detail and the installation of new equipment. Under the Borie's direction quality, which never saw the near-terminal nose-dive some estates experienced during the 20th century (escaping with merely a nasty wobble) has risen even further, and the wines today are without doubt some of the best from the Pauillac fifth-growth estates. The property is now a long-term favourite with many wise drinkers, and with the most recent vintages of all – 2009 and 2010 – quality has surpassed even previous efforts. The 2010 was without a doubt one of the top wines of the vintage when tasted from the barrel in April 2011.

The Borie family are in an enviable position in Bordeaux, holding tenure at two top estates, Ducru-Beaucaillou and Grand-Puy-Lacoste. The wines are of a top quality – for a good-value alternative look to their third estate, Château Haut-Batailley.

Château Calon-Ségur

The Calon-Ségur label features a heart, and this motif can be found at various locations around the estate. This is because onetime-proprietor, the Marquis de Ségur, was once quoted as saying "I make my wine at Lafite and Latour but my heart is in Calon".

Best recent vintage: 2009
Also worth a look: 1996

Like its near neighbour Phélan-Ségur, Calon was once part of the great Ségur estate, a substantial domaine which at one time encompassed not only Lafite but also Latour and Mouton. This was back in the 18th century, but for our purposes the story starts in the 19th century, when the estate was purchased by Georges Gasqueton and his uncle Charles Hanappier, the pair having handed over half a million francs for the château and vineyards. Although in joint ownership, it was the Gasquetons that were largely responsible for revitalising Calon-Ségur, starting with Georges in 1931 and then down through the generations to Edouard and later Philippe. When Philippe died the estate came to its modern-day doyenne, his widow Denise Capbern-Gasqueton.

Madame Capbern-Gasqueton grasped the iron with both hands and, despite being of a more mature vintage than other new proprietors in

Bordeaux, set to her new job with gusto, running the estate, supervising the vineyards and making the wine. During her tenure, quality at Calon-Ségur once again began to ascend, and the 1995 vintage seems to be considered as a turning point by many. Tasting the 1996 in its youth I was certainly taken by the substance and fruit expressed by the wine, admittedly a Médoc-wide feature of the vintage, but impressive all the same.

As well as improving the quality of the wine, Madame Capbern-Gasqueton also developed a reputation for turning away eager but unwanted visitors – I was once on the receiving end of her stonewalling, despite having an appointment to taste. Although her tenure was successful it proved to be a relatively short one, coming to an end in September 2011 (when she passed away at the very respectable age of 87) after only 16 years at the helm. With this sad event the running of the estate has passed down the female line, to her daughter Hélène and granddaughter Isabelle.

The wines were once made by one André Ellisade, but there is now a new régisseur named Vincent Millet, a graduate of the great Château Margaux, who arrived at Calon-Ségur as recently as 2006. He is fortunate enough to have an impressive array of facilities to hand, well-tended vineyards and well-equipped cellars. I am certainly looking forward to tasting more from this estate in the future, and to see in which direction the château grows and develops under the capable captaincy of Hélène Gasqueton and Vincent Millet.

Château
Palmer

Best recent vintage: 2009
Also worth a look: 2005

W hat is it about Château Palmer that foments such particularly fervent admiration amongst British drinkers of Bordeaux? Is it the estate's peculiarly British history, the château and vineyards having been in the possession (until 1843) of General Charles Palmer, who had previously served under Wellington in the British army? Or is it those dramatic labels, that intricate gold design on its bold black background, perhaps the most distinctive and virile in all Bordeaux?

No, it is of course something much more obvious than that. It is the quality, the vigour, dare I say it the pedigree, of the wines made at Palmer that regularly cause such a reaction. Château Palmer is one of a large collection – ten in all – of third growth properties located in Margaux, and in terms of sheer quality Palmer has for many years led this pack by a length, producing wine of such a high standard that it has frequently wiped the floor with the Margaux second growths. But that is not all, for this admirable track record does not only concern just one or two recent vintages. If we look back a few decades we also see the wines challenging those of the somnolent Château Margaux for the best in the appellation. Indeed, were it not for the renaissance of Château Margaux following its purchase by the Mentzelopoulos family in 1977, Palmer may well have been the top wine of the appellation today.

During the 19th and 20th centuries Palmer was is in the hands of a consortium led by four famous Bordeaux families: Sichel, Ginestet, Miailhe and Mähler-Besse. They created a

company, the Société Civile du Château Palmer, in order to manage the estate. Of this formidable foursome of Bordeaux names it was Edouard Miailhe who managed the estate, control subsequently passing to his son-in-law's family, before the Palmer shareholders elected to put a young oenologist named Thomas Duroux in charge of managing the vineyards and winemaking. To this day, it is Duroux who directs operations, especially winemaking.

Recent tastings have driven home the fact that Palmer is, most certainly, the pretender to the crown of Margaux. This was most evident in the 2008 vintage, when I traveled straight from the official Margaux tasting at the primeurs – where I tasted the majority of the cru classé estates of the commune (including the likes of Rauzan-Ségla, Durfort-Vivens and Brane-Cantenac) – to a tasting with Bernard de Laage at Palmer. The grand vin at Château Palmer wiped the floor with the other wines of the commune and, rather embarrassingly, the second wine Alter Ego did much the same. Palmer does indeed make some truly magnificent wines, and I sense a new era of excellence dawning with the arrival of Duroux, an exceptionally wise appointment by the shrewd Palmer shareholders.

Château Smith-Haut-Lafitte

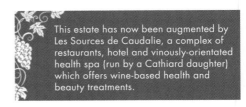

This estate has now been augmented by Les Sources de Caudalie, a complex of restaurants, hotel and vinously-orientated health spa (run by a Cathiard daughter) which offers wine-based health and beauty treatments.

Best recent vintage: 2009 for red, 2006 for white
Also worth a look: 2005 for red, 2007 for white

When my interest in the wine industry became serious, the wines of Château Smith-Haut-Lafitte had a reputation for under-performing. When looking for quality in this particular region of Bordeaux, estates such as Pape-Clément, Domaine de Chevalier, Haut-Bailly and, of course, the complex of Haut-Brion properties were considered the places to head for. Today, this view is an outdated one. Smith-Haut-Lafitte is a good example of the success reinvestment and revitalisation can achieve, and tastings of recent vintages, both white and red, have demonstrated there are now very good wines produced here. If further proof were needed, wine critic Robert Parker recently awarded the château's red wine (2009 vintage) 100 points.

In the case of Smith-Haut-Lafitte, that reinvestment and reinvigoration came courtesy of Daniel Cathiard, who acquired the estate in the 1990s. It is Cathiard, an Olympic skier who purchased the estate with the wealth generated by his chain of supermarkets, who has been credited with returning Smith-Haut-Lafitte to its former glory. Having sold their business interests, Daniel and his wife Florence

have invested heavily, restoring buildings, replacing vats and constructing a new barrel cellar. Perhaps the most striking addition to the estate is the dramatic entrance to the barrel cellar, which lies beneath a tasting room. At the press of a button the tasting-room floor opens, to reveal a secret, Bond-esque descent into the abyss.

As for the vineyards, Cathiard has moved away from mechanical and chemical influences to a more organic state. In 1992 herbicides were banned, and biological methods of pest control were introduced four years later. Harvesting and sorting methods were reviewed, and a new grape reception area was installed in 2001.

This being Pessac-Léognan, we find white and red wines here, and both have seen great improvements under the Cathiards. The white wines are fermented in small stainless steel vats, the red in large tronconic oak vats which replaced the steel vats in 2000, all under the supervision of technical director Fabien Teitgen and oenologist Yann Laudeho. The finished wines are excellent examples of the type, the white exotic and rich in fruit, the red much more stylish than the wines of old. This is a great property which lost its way last century, but in the past decade has forced its way back to prominence.

Domaine de Chevalier

Best recent vintage: 2009 for red, 2006 for white
Also worth a look: 2005 for red, 2008 for white

Domaine de Chevalier hides in a pine forest on the western edge of the region known since 1987 as Pessac-Léognan, the most northerly vineyards of Graves. Although many châteaux in the southern Médoc and Graves have centuries of history, this property dates from only the 18th century, and viticulture was only significantly developed at the estate during the 19th century (although the very first vines were planted long before that). As Bordeaux expanded and the Médoc was drained, opening up the gravelly terroirs of the left bank, one entrepreneur looked south instead of north to establish his vineyard, and Domaine de Chevalier was born.

Jean Ricard, a local cooper, first extended the small vineyard in the late-19th century, but it was his son-in-law Gabriel Beaumartin, taking control after Ricard's death in 1900, who began to build up the quality and reputation of the wine. The property remained with the Ricard family until 1983, eventually under the guidance of Claude Ricard who had gained control in 1948, and who saw Domaine de Chevalier produce some of its

greatest wines – both red and white – during the mid-20th century. Due to inheritance difficulties – inheriting a family-owned property in Bordeaux can be an expensive business – Domaine de Chevalier was eventually sold and passed into the hands of Olivier Bernard.

The estate produces both red and white wines, as per the 1959 Graves classification. Having tasted more than a few vintages of both, I feel quality here is not only very strong, but also seems to be continually improving. These are structured, classically styled wines which need cellar time, and do not necessarily flatter with plump fruit early on in their development. And whereas there are many estates that tend to be stronger on either the red or the white wine, at Domaine de Chevalier both can be supreme. Recent vintages such as 2006 show the fabulous appeal that the white can offer, but there have been many other vintages of note, and the same can be said for the red. My opinion is that these are, without doubt, wines to buy with confidence.

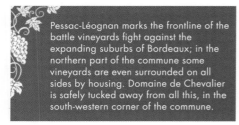

Pessac-Léognan marks the frontline of the battle vineyards fight against the expanding suburbs of Bordeaux; in the northern part of the commune some vineyards are even surrounded on all sides by housing. Domaine de Chevalier is safely tucked away from all this, in the south-western corner of the commune.

Château Angélus

Best recent vintage: **2009**
Also worth a look: **2005**

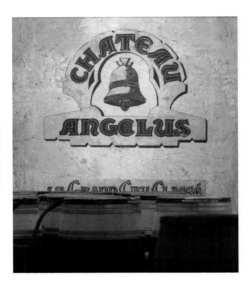

The history of Angélus is inextricably intertwined with that of the Boüard de Laforest family, who have been patrons of the estate since the early 20th century. They acquired the vineyards in 1909, when Comte Maurice de Boüard de Laforest was bequeathed the Domaine de Mazerat, part of the estate belonging to his aunt, who was a Souffrain (a large landowning family that held sway over vast areas of St Emilion at that time). This small acquisition was added to in 1924 and again in 1969, the eventual combination of the three vineyards giving us the Angélus we know today.

The estate is currently run and managed by Hubert de Boüard de Laforest, who had studied under the great Emile Peynaud at the Faculté d'Oenologie in Bordeaux, as well gaining a few years of experience at Château Thieuley with Francis Courselle. He had also – somewhat unusually – spent some time in distant Burgundy. Joining the family business in 1976 he soon realised that there was considerable room for improvement in practically all areas at Angélus, in both the vineyard and the cellars, and it was not long before Hubert initiated a program of

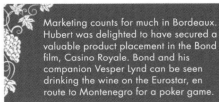

Marketing counts for much in Bordeaux. Hubert was delighted to have secured a valuable product placement in the Bond film, Casino Royale. Bond and his companion Vesper Lynd can be seen drinking the wine on the Eurostar, en route to Montenegro for a poker game.

investment and refurbishment.

He started with the introduction of new equipment, stainless steel to replace the vinification vessels which were previously concrete, and new barrels for the subsequent maturation of the wines. Following Hubert taking full control in 1985, Angélus has also seen the arrival of climate-controlled cellars and a new tasting room. Perhaps more notably, some of his experiences in Burgundy have been incorporated into the winemaking at Angélus, such as the rapid transfer of the wine into barrel, where malolactic occurs, and the importance of lees in the élevage of red wines. These changes may sound relatively minor, but when one considers that Hubert de Boüard's father never utilised barrel maturation at all, the wine going straight from concrete tank to bottle, this marked a major shift in direction (and a huge financial investment) for Angélus.

As a result this estate has come on leaps and bounds, the wines displaying a tangible escalation in quality not just in great vintages (2005 and 2009) but also in more challenging years, such as 2006 or 2003. Boüard's energy and investment has also brought classification success, the estate seeing elevation from Grand Cru Classé to Premier Grand Cru Classé B status in 1996. Who knows what will happen when the classification is next revised?

Vieux
Château Certan

Best recent vintage: 2010
Also worth a look: 2008

The Thienpont family, originally from Belgium, are another of the great Bordeaux dynasties to be aware of. Alexandre's cousin, Jacques, is in charge at nearby Le Pin, source of one of Bordeaux's most expensive wines.

Vieux Château Certan provided me with one of those rare vinous experiences when, on first contact with the wine, I fell instantly in love. It was at a mini-vertical tasting of the wines, where we looked at six vintages from the property, taking in acclaimed (or at least good) right bank vintages such as 1995 and 1989, but also years not considered choice – 1993 and 1975, for instance. From the better years the wines were seductive and hedonistic, yet also complex and structured, fresh and lively. More tellingly, however, the wines from the less exalted vintages also wowed, and if there's any sign of an excellent estate and terroir, this is it. Ever since then, right up to the most recent of vintages, I have been an ardent admirer of the wines made at Vieux Château Certan.

The modern history of the estate begins with its acquisition by Georges Thienpont in 1924. Georges also owned Château Troplong-Mondot in St Emilion, but as a consequence of the depression and war that ravaged the early 20th century, he was forced to sell one of his estates. As Troplong was the more profitable and the more attractive to any potential buyer, it was sold, leaving Thienpont with Vieux Château Certan. It was not, in the long run, a bad decision. Following World War II Georges and his son Léon poured their time and money into the estate, and the château became a source of fabulous wines. This quality continues into modern times, Alexandre Thienpont having taken control after Léon's death in 1985.

Under the watchful gaze of the cerebral Alexandre, the quality of wines produced by Vieux Château Certan has again soared. As my tasting experience has indicated to me, these wines are some of the most delicious in Bordeaux, never mind Pomerol alone. Alexandre's commitment shows through in the wines; these are sourced from 14 hectares of vines planted in a single block, the varieties employed being 60% Merlot, 30% Cabernet Franc and 10% Cabernet Sauvignon, although the eventual blend is typically dominated by Merlot at 75-80%. In some recent vintages the Cabernet Franc has struggled, and the wine is even more dependent on Merlot. This may influence the style of the wine, but quality has never faltered. Time and time again Vieux Château Certan proves its worth; the wines have a deep colour, complexity and a velvety texture, and are integrated with a fine structure which belies the significant role Cabernet Franc and Cabernet Sauvignon play in the wine. I think it's perhaps this latter aspect that I find so appealing, but in fact it's the whole package that makes these wines so brilliant.

Château Haut-Bailly

The grounds of Château Haut-Bailly boast a sculpture by renowned artist Bernar Venet, whose work also features on the 2007 label of Château Mouton-Rothschild.

Best recent vintage: 2009
Also worth a look: 1996

T he origins of Château Haut-Bailly lie in the 16th century when the vineyard was established by rich merchants from the Pays Basque region, to the south of Bordeaux. Nevertheless, the most celebrated proprietor of old was probably Alcide Bellot des Minières, who acquired the estate in 1872. He reorganised and expanded the vineyards before building the château, which still stands today. The wine's reputation grew, and prices easily matched those of a deuxième cru from further north. Flushed with this success, Bellot des Minières famously described his wine as a Premier Grand Cru Exceptionnel, and the term Cru Exceptionnel can be found on the Haut-Bailly label as recently as the 1985 vintage, only disappearing in 1986.

Despite these early successes, by the mid-20th century the estate was floundering, the vineyards were in a state, and the reputation of the wines had plummeted. It was the sale of the property in 1955 to Daniel Sanders, a Belgian born into a family of linen merchants, that was to save the estate. Despite grafting for many years, by the time he handed over the running of the estate to the next generation in 1979 there was still much work to do. His son Jean took the reins, but

when his sisters insisted upon selling their share of the estate, it seemed as though the family would lose control of the property for good. Indeed, it was acquired by Robert Wilmers, an American banker. He has always taken a back seat, yet within a few years Daniel retired to be replaced by his daughter Véronique. This situation still stands today, Véronique being the charming face of the modern Haut-Bailly.

Wilmers bankrolled everything; from an extensive geological survey of the vineyards and purchases of new equipment, to hiring the services of high-profile consultants (including Jean-Bernard Delmas, associated in recent times with Montrose, but for many years closely affiliated with Haut-Brion). Perhaps a consultant of such vinous gravitas is appropriate; I learnt during a visit to Haut-Bailly in early 2010 that over a century ago the wines were sold alongside the celebrated Haut-Brion, and the property was at that time held in a similar regard. As for today's wines, quality here is higher than ever, although like a number of other properties across Bordeaux – some would say almost all properties across the region – there has been a change in style. The wines are not as restrained as they once were, and there is a new focus on concentration and substance over subtlety and refinement. The 2009 is a case in point; I found it particularly dark and brooding when I first tasted from the barrel in 2010...a wine of real presence that has maintained this compact power into the bottle. It is a fabulous wine in the modern Bordeaux style, although I am aware it will not appeal to some Haut-Bailly drinkers of the old school.

Château Église-Clinet

Best recent vintage: 2010
Also worth a look: 2009

C an there be a more complex interweaving of vinous families and names than in Pomerol, with all its Lafleurs, Églises, Clinets and Gazins? It is a system that seems designed to befuddle, although a visit to the region can do much to clear the fog of confusion. Every time I walk across the vineyards of Pomerol, or drive from one property to the next, I broaden by just a little my understanding of the panoply of Pomerol estates, how they have evolved, and how they are related to one another. Château L'Église-Clinet is a prime example of one of these 'blended' names, and like many properties in Pomerol it is, put blandly, nothing to look at. I have lost count of the number of times I have snapped away at a roadside property, only to subsequently find – using online satellite mapping – that it was some exalted estate, such as Lafleur-Gazin or indeed Lafleur itself. Whilst L'Église-Clinet might not be 'roadside', it still maintains an anonymity that can add a frisson of excitement when trying to locate it, especially when you are already late for your primeur tasting appointment!

The ecclesiastical église component of the property's name reflects the presence not of the modern-day church in Pomerol, but of a more ancient chapel, one that dated to perhaps the 12th century. The Clinet was added sometime in the 19th century, when the estate was in the ownership of the Constant family, who also owned nearby Château Clinet. From them it passed to the Rouchut family, and eventually to the current proprietor Denis Durantou. He did not take the reins at the estate until 1983,

following a period during which the property was run by his elders, with the help of manager Pierre Lasserre. Lasserre had used largely outdated techniques, so with the introduction of new equipment and practises, including lowering the yield at harvest, Durantou was able to push the wine's quality to new levels.

Today Durantou manages not only L'Église-Clinet, a leading Pomerol estate with a fine reputation (cemented solely by himself, it must be said), but also a small portfolio of vineyards in a variety of right bank appellations, including La Chenade and Les Cruzelles (both estates in Lalande de Pomerol), Saintayme (in St Emilion) and Montlandrie (in Castillon). Any visit to the property will see you tasting all of these wines; and they should not be overlooked, for there is a great deal of good value to be found here. But the real draw remains the wines of Église-Clinet itself; Petrus and Le Pin may be wines to obsess over, and if you're lucky taste occasionally, but if you're after a more affordable wine for drinking, it is to properties such as Église-Clinet that you should turn.

1995

CHATEAU PALMER

MARGAUX

APPELLATION MARGAUX CONTRÔLÉE

SOCIÉTÉ CIVILE DU CHÂTEAU PALMER, MARGAUX . FR

MIS EN BOUTEILLE AU CHÂTEAU

Mähler-Bess

6

Top 5 Sauternes

Although Bordeaux is most famous for its red wines, we must never overlook the distinctively delicious wines of Sauternes. These wines owe their existence to Noble Rot, a fungus which shrivels and dries the grapes, thereby concentrating the sugars and all the other flavour elements as well. Relatively under-appreciated these days (apart from the mighty Yquem, dealt with on page 39), these fabulous wines remain under-valued. Buy them while you still can!

Château Climens

Best recent vintage: **2011**
Also worth a look: **2001**

There are few more distinctive properties in the Sauternes and Barsac appellations than Climens. The château certainly has a distinctive appearance, sitting atop a very low rise just to the south-west of Coutet and Doisy-Daëne, the single-story chartreuse-style villa flanked at either end by rectangular towers, each one topped by a slate pyramid roof. The current proprietor, Bérénice Lurton, also has a distinctive approach; there are no primeur samples here, for instance. Not only does she not participate in the Union des Grands Crus tastings at this stage, but a visit to the property will not yield a taste of a final or even a proposed blend, but rather a barrel-by-barrel tasting of potential components, more akin to what you might find when visiting a small grower in the Loire Valley than a big-name Bordeaux château. And as for the wine itself, no-one can deny that it has a distinctive character, with a fresh Barsac acidity and great depth of botrytised-fruit. In my opinion this is one of the two top addresses in Barsac (although there are a good number of delicious wines made throughout the commune).

Château Climens has a lengthy and fairly well documented history stretching back perhaps 500

years, although it does not seem that viticulture was undertaken here until the 17th century. The Roborel family were early proprietors, and later the Gounouilhou family, before it was acquired by Lucien Lurton in 1971. Subsequently it was passed to Bérénice, the youngest of Lucien's ten children. At the time of her taking the reins at Château Climens she was barely out of university, aged just 22 years. It was something of a baptism of fire, and although the 1989 and 1990 vintages had been relatively kind, the most recent vintages before she took control – 1991 and 1992 – were both dismal. Then came 1993 and 1994, neither of which will go down in the annals of great Sauternes vintages, particularly the latter, which was a washout for the commune as a whole.

Nevertheless, by the time Bérénice took control of the estate Climens had gained a strong reputation. She would claim her contribution has been to merely fine tune things, rather than invoke a quality revolution. Having said that, significant changes were made, including better tracking of fruit from plot of origin through to fermentation, which facilitates a better understanding of the vineyard and future selection, as well as introducing a sorting table at harvest time. She remains a passionate advocate for the region and for the château, and is not afraid to travel within France and abroad to show her wines, which are among the very best – if, in fact, the actual best – of all Sauternes and Barsac.

> The commune of Barsac has its own appellation – Barsac – but the wines may also be classified as Sauternes. Unusually, the proprietors have a choice of which to use. Both Climens and Coutet, the two top estates, opt for Barsac.

Château Coutet

Best recent vintage: **2011**
Also worth a look: **2007**

The history of Château Coutet dates back to the 13th century, hundreds of years before anyone even dreamt of planting vines on the then-marshy, now-prosperous Médoc. Some parts of the château date from that period, as is obvious from the most perfunctory examination of the property; these parts have thick walls of stone, rounded towers and defensive castellations. There has, however, been extensive augmentation over the ensuing centuries, including a 14th-century chapel, two 16th-century towers and further remodelling in the 18th century. The most recent additions have a much finer appearance than the early parts, with slate roofs. The château boasts a dramatic blend of both ancient and modern. In a way this is a good analogy for the family that run the estate and the wine they make; there is no shortage of awareness of the heritage of the estate and Sauternes, but with a bright new generation grasping the helm this is an estate disposed to looking forward rather than back.

The Lur-Saluces family – best known for their long tenure, recently ended, at Yquem – maintained control of Coutet for over a century, but by 1922 production had dropped off and the estate was sold. It passed through a number of hands before it was acquired by the Baly family, originally from Alsace. It was Marcel Baly that made the purchase, although it has since been

The soils of Barsac are distinctive, with a rich red clay over a deeper limestone seam peppered with fossils of starfish and shellfish. It is these soils that are usually credited with giving the wines their trademark fresh acidity.

passed onto his sons, Dominique and Philippe, with the latter playing a more prominent role. The vineyard was not in tip-top condition when they moved in, and the wines were certainly less than ideal, being rather lighter and more delicate than we would expect today. There was a lot of work required initially in the vineyard, with extensive replanting, and then also in the cellars. It was a decade before the benefits of their labours became tangible, and I have long been an ardent admirer of the 1989, which was one of the first Baly vintages to show what this vineyard is really capable of.

In 1994 the Baly family signed a distribution deal with Baron Philippe de Rothschild SA, and so these days wherever you find Mouton-Rothschild you are likely to find Coutet. One great benefit of this relationship was that the deal included technical advice from the technical director at Mouton, Patrick Léon. More recently it has been Philippe Dhalluin who has filled this role, and it seems to me that these two individuals should take some of the credit for the continued improvement in quality of Château Coutet wine. In more recent years Philippe has also been joined by his niece Aline Baly, who was educated in the USA. Together this team are turning out some magnificent wines, rich and yet bright, and along with Climens they are some of the best the commune has to offer.

Château Rieussec

Best recent vintage: 2011
Also worth a look: 2007

The history of this illustrious Sauternes estate, which is located in the commune of Fargues very close indeed to Yquem, stretches back many centuries, to when the estate was in the ownership of Carmelite monks. The origin of the name Rieussec remains uncertain, although it may be derived from Ruisseau, the name of a stream which runs between Rieussec and Yquem, and '...sec', the latter part of the word, applied because the stream is known to dry up during the summer months.

Following the French Revolution the estate passed through the hands of a long succession of proprietors and was ultimately acquired by French supermarket magnate Albert Vuillier in the mid-20th century. At first Vuillier was an absentee landlord, but in 1974 he moved into the château and took charge. By all accounts he was prepared to invest heavily, with replanting some of the rundown vineyards high on his agenda, but he soon found that such investment was simply not feasible. A string of unsuccessful vintages, coupled with low demand for the wines, meant that he soon needed help. It came, in 1984, in the form of the Rothschilds. Initially Alain Vuillier stayed on, but in 1985 he was replaced as manager of the estate by Charles Chevalier, who now also

runs the show at Lafite. Under the direction of Chevalier, and with the financial clout of the Rothschild family, there has been continued investment and revitalisation at Rieussec, and I think it is fair to say that the estate now sits comfortably among the top producers of Sauternes.

The vineyards occupy one of the highest points in Sauternes after those of Yquem which are adjacent, to the east. The Rothschild investment is mainly evident in the cellars, which are very well equipped. The fruit is fermented in barrels allowing for a small-batch approach, so that each plot of vines can be individually managed and subsequently assessed. Alongside the grand vin there is a second wine, Carmes de Rieussec, named for the monks that once owned the estate. The first wine is excellent, and much of this can be attributed to the investment put in place by the Rothschild family, with the efforts of Chevalier on the shop floor. The style of wine they and Chevalier produce tends to be one of concentration with elegance, whereas older vintages, under Vuillier, tended towards a voluptuous and fat nature – the wines of the Chevalier era are the ones to go for.

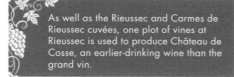

As well as the Rieussec and Carmes de Rieussec cuvées, one plot of vines at Rieussec is used to produce Château de Cosse, an earlier-drinking wine than the grand vin.

Château
Suduiraut

Best recent vintage: 2011
Also worth a look: 2007

Château Suduiraut is one of several Sauternes châteaux to include a dry white, named S de Suduiraut, in their portfolio. Fruit that hasn't been made sweet by botrytis, often picked early for this very purpose, goes into this wine.

This property was once the dominion of the Suduiraut family who resided here during the 16th century. At one point they fell foul of the local Governor, the Duc d'Epernon, who exacted his revenge by flattening their property, ultimately forcing the family to redesign and rebuild. In the process the Comte Blaise de Suduiraut created one of the finest properties in all Bordeaux, surrounding his pristine and elegant two-storey château with an expanse of gardens. As a result, today the château stands in a large area of parkland ringed by trees, the vineyards situated on either side of the lengthy driveway that scythes up to the buildings.

By the early 20th century the property had come upon hard times, but the regeneration it required was kick-started by the industrialist

Leopold-Francois Fonquernie. Aided by manager Pierre Pascaud, Fonquernie instituted a program of renovation and improvement for both the vineyards and the cellars. Following his death the estate was eventually acquired by AXA Millésimes in 1992, the wine subsidiary of the AXA insurance group. AXA have been instrumental in the revitalisation of other top Bordeaux properties including Château Pichon-Baron. Throughout this time Pierre Pascaud stayed on at the château, although he was ultimately replaced by Christian Seely, who oversees work at all the AXA properties in France and abroad, ably assisted by technical director Pierre Montégut.

Recent tastings of Suduiraut show that this is a property currently on a roll; the wines in the most recent vintages have been at least very good, and some have proved truly excellent. The 2001 is without a doubt a great wine, and although I was once troubled by a little volatile acidity on one particular assessment, subsequent tastes showed this to be a one-off issue, most likely isolated to that single bottle. With more recent vintages showing exceptional quality, Château Suduiraut is now one of the leading estates of the appellation in my opinion.

Château Lafaurie-Peyraguey

Best recent vintage: **2011**
Also worth a look: **2007**

Lafaurie-Peyraguey can trace its history back at least seven centuries. The construction of a fortified keep in the 13th century, using stone quarried from nearby Ciron, is perhaps the earliest indication of the significance of the site, although this precedes the arrival of viticulture by a significant period of time indeed. It was not really until the 17th and 18th centuries that the vine arrived, with Sieur Raymond Peyraguey being instrumental in this, although a stronger driving force in moving the property towards ordered viticulture was Baron Nicolas-Pierre de Pichard, who acquired the estate in 1742.

What was then known as Pichard-Peyraguey was acquired by Monsieur Lafaurie in 1796; previously a lowly ranked estate, within half a century (or thereabouts) Lafaurie-Peyraguey was one of the top names for Sauternes, a favoured tipple of King Alphonso XII of Spain, and was ranked third in the 1855 classification of Sauternes and Barsac, directly behind Yquem and La Tour Blanche. Following Lafaurie's death it came to Comte Duchâtel in 1865, who remodelled the château and thus is responsible for much of the estate's appearence today. Under subsequent

owners quality deteriorated, however, and it was not until the Cordier family intervened, acquiring the estate in 1917, that things changed for the better. This has continued under the current owners, GDF Suez, who acquired the property and vineyards in 1984.

The 1986 vintage was a turning point for Lafaurie-Peyraguey, one that indicated the estate was clearly on the up following the installation of Yannick Laporte as régisseur in 1983, and no doubt also influenced by new direction (and investment) from GDF Suez. Other more recent vintages, under director and oenologist Eric Larramona are no less wonderful; both the 2001 and 2003 look stunning, and the 2007 has the same potential. Lafaurie-Peyraguey's future is looking very bright.

> Lafaurie-Peyraguey's close neighbour Clos Haut-Peyraguey is also worth a taste, although the wines can be a little harder to track down than those of its illustrious neighbour.

7

Top 10 Value

As prices of top Bordeaux seem set to climb ever higher, knowledge of under-rated châteaux, such as the ten here, is essential. Some winemakers, such as Jean-Christophe Mau at Château Brown, seem determined to continue turning out superb wines to challenge more highly ranked châteaux, while maintaining very favourable prices. The wines recommended here are not necessarily 'cheap' – but they all promise super value for your money.

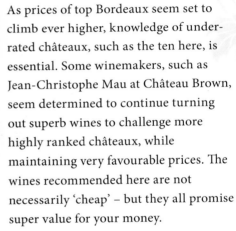

Château Sociando-Mallet

Best recent vintage: 2009
Also worth a look: 2005

Sociando-Mallet is one of those châteaux which makes a mockery of the 1855 classification of Bordeaux. Never entered into the classification of cru classé châteaux, and subsequently classified as a cru bourgeois estate in 1932, it consistently turns out wines which outshine those produced by many of its more illustrious neighbours. This apparent omission from the 1855 classification was further highlighted in 2003 when the ill-fated cru bourgeois classification was revised. Sociando-Mallet was now nowhere to be seen – the confident Jean Gautreau opted to remain outside of this system, perhaps feeling that participation would actually lower the standing of his château, but perhaps also discouraged by some of the petty politics that seemed to surround the process. Politics which ultimately resulted in the farcical collapse of the entire classification.

The history of Sociando-Mallet extends back at least as far as the early 17th century, as records reveal that the estate was the residence of a Basque nobleman named Sociando in 1633. Otherwise the ancient history of the estate is sketchy. When Gautreau acquired Sociando-Mallet in 1969 it was a somewhat dilapidated property – one perhaps purchased more with the heart, rather than the head. Those vineyards that had fallen out of use were ploughed, revealing promising gravelly soils, typical of the vineyards that run along the banks of the Gironde. Gautreau would say it is this terroir, the same band of gravel that runs through Latour and numerous other leading properties of the Médoc, that gives the wines of Sociando-Mallet their fine character.

During his tenure Jean Gautreau has been a meticulous guardian of Sociando-Mallet, and has elevated the quality so that the estate now ranks alongside many other cru classé châteaux. Talking with Gautreau reveals which châteaux he sees as members of his peer group; they include certain troisième cru estates, such as Giscours, although I feel that truthfully he may set his sights a little higher than this. There have been over four decades of investment and firm direction at Sociando-Mallet, and the resulting wines are excellent. They have a pure, cool style which oozes class, rather than the rustic charm and less well delineated palate that characterises other estates of the Haut-Médoc. Nevertheless, no matter how brilliant the wines are now, I think this is an estate still with plenty to come, and that Gautreau – and his daughter, set to succeed him – would like to squeeze another few drops of excellence from the fruit they harvest.

It is often said that any estate with a good view of the Gironde, the estuary fed by the Dordogne and the Garonne, can make great wine, an assertion which is related to the fine gravelly soils this close to the water. The view from Sociando-Mallet's recently constructed tasting room affords just such a view.

Château
Cantemerle

Best recent vintage: 2005
Also worth a look: 2000

There are several Bordeaux châteaux that have played an important role in the understanding of the major vine diseases, and have helped develop treatments for them. Cantemerle is one of them, as sulphur-dusting for powdery mildew was first tested here.

The origins of what we know today as Château Cantemerle lie in the Middle Ages, when the château formed one part of the Médoc's defensive line against attack. Exactly how the name Cantemerle came into existence, however, is open to debate. Various fanciful stories exist, the least incredulous of which concerns a large cannon named Merle; such armoury would not be unusual on a fortified battlement of the Middle Ages. Whatever the origins of the name, by the mid-13th century Cantemerle is an important stronghold in the region, complete with resident knight, Pons de Cantemerle, who fought on the side of the English at the Battle of Taillebourg in 1242.

The first evidence of viticulture at Cantemerle is from 1354, when the owner, Ponset de Cantemerle, was recorded as paying a debt with a tonneau of clairet (the origin of the word claret), essentially a barrel of the local wine. The estate then passed through the hands of several different families during the ensuing years, coming to the Villeneuves and then the Durforts, and finally the Dubros family before it came into the ownership, in 1981, of Groupe SMABTP, a financial group offering pension and insurance services. Such big business ownership is quite the norm in Bordeaux these days, but at least these large firms are in a financial position to put in place the required investment for renovation that many estates desperately need. Taking charge on behalf of SMABTP are Phillippe Dambrine and cellar master Pascal Berteau.

The wines, in my experience, represent extremely good value. They offer a winning combination of good quality – in keeping with a fifth growth château – and sensible pricing. I've long held a soft spot for the 1996 vintage, but tasting more recent vintages only confirms my belief that this is a good value property that only committed label-drinkers should overlook. If purchased at the right price, and (crucially) stored correctly, Cantemerle will offer you decades of drinking pleasure.

Château Gloria

Best recent vintage: 2010
Also worth a look: 2009

Château Gloria is something of an anomaly in Bordeaux. It has no official place in the 1855 classification, because it did not exist at that time. It came into being as the result of one man's desire to own and run a classed growth property. That man was one-time mayor of St Julien, Henri Martin. Born at Château Gruaud-Larose in 1903 it seems as though Martin was born into wine. His grandfather was the cellar-master there, and his father Alfred was a barrel maker both at Gruaud-Larose and Château Saint-Pierre. When the proprietor of Saint-Pierre died the Martin family scraped enough together to purchase a small plot of vines from the estate, and the barrel room from which he ran his barrel-making activities. He remained here until 1936 when, following a strike held by his staff, Alfred sold his business and became a grocer instead. It seemed as though the Martin family were to be divorced from wine forever.

But this was not to be. In 1942, encouraged by Jean-Charles Cazes of Lynch-Bages, Henri Martin purchased 6 hectares of vines in St Julien. This was the beginning of Château Gloria, the name coming from the land on which the Martin family home was built. Over the years the vineyard expanded to a very respectable 48 hectares, augmented by parcels from numerous classed growth neighbours. The reputation of the wine also grew, becoming a popular choice for those interested in quality and not just posh labels. Martin died in 1991, but not before he realised his ambition to own a classed growth château, which he achieved with the purchase of the aforementioned Saint-Pierre in 1982. Today his son-in-law, Jean-Louis Triaud, continues his work at both estates.

The wines of Gloria receive mixed reviews. These are wines made from the fruit of St Julien vineyards, but I don't think anyone is expecting them to match the top estates from this commune. Nevertheless, the Gloria label indicates a well made wine that drinks well in many vintages. Tasting older examples, such as the 1982, shows that not only is the requisite quality there, but so is the ability to age. In more recent vintages Triaud really seems to have been pushing the envelope hard, both here and at Saint-Pierre. Although I would have once described the wines as worthy, having tasted the 2010 from the barrel (which has attained a quality never before seen at Gloria, it must be said) there is potential here for both optimism and excitement, as well as good value.

> For many years Henri Martin often set the scene on the Bordeaux place, where the wines are traded, by being the first to release prices for the latest vintage of his wine, usually announced prior to any of the classed growth estates.

Château Brown

Best recent vintage: 2009 for red, 2011 for white
Also worth a look: 2007 for white, 2005 for red

There are innumerable châteaux in Bordeaux that bear testament to the presence of the British in the region. One such Briton was John Lewis Brown, a wealthy Scottish trader who settled in Bordeaux near the end of the 18th century; his name lives on not only in the Médoc, at Château Cantenac-Brown, but also down near Léognan, in the shape of Château Brown. The wines of Château Brown enjoyed an admirable reputation during the 19th century, and stood up well against their peers. Nevertheless, during the early 20th century the estate fell into disrepair, and eventually ceased to function as a vineyard. With the advancing sprawl of the city of Bordeaux, it's a wonder the vineyard did not disappear altogether.

In 1939 the estate was purchased by André Bonnel, and it was under his tenure that the viticulture stopped. Twenty years later the vineyard was rescued and replanted, but it was too late for the property to take its place in the Graves Classification of 1953. Although many say these classifications are today irrelevant (and I would not put up too much of a counter-argument) failure to be ranked – often down to timing and politics as much as quality – is a recurring theme when finding hidden gems such as Château Brown. The estate passed from the Bonnel family to Bernard Barthe, who poured effort and investment into the estate, as evinced by

> The Mau family run one of the largest Bordeaux négociant firms, and are still the company behind many supermarket-level Bordeaux wines. But the acquisition of Château Brown, and also Château Preuillac in the Médoc, marks a move toward a higher quality level.

the gleaming cellars, temperature-controlled stainless steel vats of varying sizes and a state-of-the-art pneumatic press. Yet the true renaissance for Brown was still to come, and it was only with the arrival of Jean-Christophe Mau, from a famous Bordeaux family, in conjunction with the Dutch Dirkzweger family, that the real rescue began.

Top Bordeaux consultant Stéphane Derenoncourt was engaged to advise on the wine, and immediately the quality improved. Although I have tasted one or two more mature vintages, it is the wines of the Mau-Derenoncourt era that are worth tracking down, starting particularly with the superlative 2005 and the drastically under-rated 2004 vintage. Remarkably, Mau has not increased the release price of Brown on the Bordeaux place, despite the investment and obvious improvement that is apparent in the wines, both white and red. Clearly, now is a good time to be buying Château Brown.

GRAND VIN DE GRAVES

CHATEAU
BROWN

PESSAC-LÉOGNAN

Château Chasse-Spleen

Best recent vintage: 2005
Also worth a look: 2008

The Merlaut-Villars family own a significant number of left-bank Bordeaux châteaux, including Gruaud-Larose, Ferrière, La Gurgue, Citran and Haut-Bages-Liberal.

Château Chasse-Spleen is the leading estate of Moulis, a small and easily overlooked commune on the left bank of the Gironde, sandwiched in the No Man's Land between St Julien to the north and Margaux to the south. There have been vines on the estate since at least 1560, but when some of the vines were absorbed into a larger estate, what was to become Chasse-Spleen lost any sense of identity. It eventually emerged as an independent property in the 1860s, years after the 1855 classification had been drawn up.

How the estate came to be named is surrounded by an aura of myth and legend, with two popular theories competing. The first suggests that the name originated from a poem, Spleen, by Charles Baudelaire, who visited the estate when staying with his friend Odilon Redon, who was a neighbour of Chasse-Spleen. Alternatively, Lord Byron is credited with the comment that his visit there, during a journey from London to Seville, did wonders for his mood, a "remède pour chasser le spleen". Whichever of these fancy tales appeals most, by the turn of the century Chasse-Spleen was a well established Bordeaux estate in its own right.

Up until 1909 the property was owned by the Castaing family, at which point it was sold to the German firm of Seigneitz. It survived World War One, although not completely without incident; those that worked the harvest were

regarded as colluding with the enemy, and in 1914 the cellar was ransacked and all the wine stolen. In 1922 the property was sold at auction to Frank Lahary, who then passed it onto his daughter and her husband. The Lahary family steered the property through difficult times, but in the early 1970s they sold it on, the purchaser this time being Jacques Merlaut. He handed control to his daughter Bernadette Villars, and her husband, in 1976. Bernadette and her husband died tragically young, in a hiking accident in 1992, and today the estate remains under the guidance of one of their daughters, Claire Villars.

My experience with Chasse-Spleen largely concerns the very recent vintages, made by Claire, but do not shy away from more mature wines from Bernadette's era. The 1989, for example, is still going strong, mature and yet with plenty of vibrancy and vigour. The 2005 is perhaps the most successful of recent vintages.

Château Angludet

Best recent vintage: 2009
Also worth a look: 2010

The origins of Château Angludet lie in the 12th century, possibly before, when there was a manor house on the site. In its early years the estate was in the ownership of a certain knight named Bernard d'Angludet, hence the origin of its modern name. There were no vineyards then of course, but by 1776, when the estate was in the hands of Pierre Legas, viticulture was well established. The wine also had a very good reputation, but as the estate passed from one generation to the next, being gradually divided as it went, it seems to have lost some of its lustre. At its apogee the authors of the time refer to Angludet as a fourth growth, but with its deterioration over the years it slipped out of view of the relevant commentators, and when the 1855 classification was drawn up, it was nowhere to be seen. Château Angludet was forever relegated to the ranks of the cru bourgeois. This was bad news for subsequent proprietors perhaps, but good news for those who buy on taste and quality rather than labels or outmoded classifications.

During the 20th century the estate was passed from one proprietor to the next rather like a hot potato. As a result a seemingly interminable decline set in and it was not until the purchase of the estate by Peter Sichel, who owned part of Château Palmer and apparently stumbled across

the near-ruin that was Angludet on an afternoon stroll in 1961, that its fortunes were reversed. Peter, followed by his son Benjamin who took charge in 1989, gradually rebuilt the vineyards. They are managed with minimal recourse to chemical treatments, a method Benjamin Sichel described as measured prevention, planting grass between the rows to discourage weeds and to provide surface competition for the vines, a common technique today.

The wines of Angludet are not ones that tend to garner high praise, from some quarters at least. These are classically styled wines, neither opulent or seductive. Rather they are firm, only yielding with time, and eventually giving (in some cases) a mature, admirable, spicy style, while in other cases remaining rigid, muscular and hard. They are wines that can give much pleasure to those who know what to expect, and who know their own preferences. They can be rounded, meaty and attractive with the right amount of age, in the right vintage. Having found this with a number of mature and maturing vintages, such as the 1982, the 1983, the 1988 and the 1989, I look forward to more recent vintages taking on a similar, full and pleasing character given time.

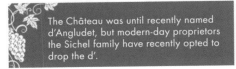

The Château was until recently named d'Angludet, but modern-day proprietors the Sichel family have recently opted to drop the d'.

Château Grand Mayne

Best recent vintage: 2008
Also worth a look: 2005

Soils are everything on the right bank, just as they are on the left. In St Emilion, the limestone and clay of the plateau of St Emilion is where all but a couple of the leading vineyards are to be found.

Château Grand Mayne is one of many estates which show that there is life outside of the premier grand cru classé ranking of St Emilion. This property has an enviable history which stretches back for more than five centuries. Originally a grand manor (it is said that this is the origin of Grand Mayne, which has been the estate's name since the 19th century), the buildings date from the latter years of the 15th and 16th centuries. As a consequence of Napoleon's inheritance laws the domaine was broken up, and the heart of the property, amounting to just 21 hectares, was to become what we know today as Château Grand Mayne.

This nubbin of the once grand domaine passed from pillar to post, through the hands of several different families, and it was not until 1934 that the current owners arrived on the scene in the shape of Jean Nony. Clearly playing the long game, he acquired the estate at a favourable price,

a result of the global economic depression of the era. He managed the estate single-handed until 1977, when his son Jean-Pierre Nony took the reins. With the death of Jean-Pierre in 2001, his widow Marie-Françoise Nony has been in charge, increasingly assisted by her sons Jean Antoine and Damien. Today, these two brothers are the face of Grand Mayne.

The vineyards are to the west of St Emilion, at the foot of the limestone plateau. It is here, on the southwest facing slopes, that the more desirable clay and limestone soils are found, with just a few vines planted on the less sought-after sandy soils at the base. There are 19 hectares of vines altogether, of which 17 hectares are planted in a single block which qualify for the grand cru classé classification. The wines that come from these vines are well worth seeking out, as amongst the châteaux ranked at this level, Grand Mayne is without doubt one of the more notable. The 1998 has been consistently impressive, and more recent vintages hold a lot of promise.

Château
Ormes de Pez

Best recent vintage: 2009
Also worth a look: 2010

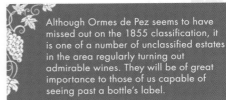

Although Ormes de Pez seems to have missed out on the 1855 classification, it is one of a number of unclassified estates in the area regularly turning out admirable wines. They will be of great importance to those of us capable of seeing past a bottle's label.

hâteau Ormes de Pez takes its name from the village of Pez near St Estèphe, as do the other nearby cru bourgeois properties of de Pez and La Tour de Pez. Ormes translates as elms, and betrays the presence of a copse of these trees, long since disappeared, near the château.

The earliest records concerning the property inform us that during the 19th century it was owned by Marcel Alibert, a local councillor, who was also the proprietor of the fifth growth Haut-Médoc estate Château Belgrave, just west of St Julien. Alibert sold Ormes de Pez in 1927 to the Société Civile du Haut Médoc, but it quickly passed to the brokers Louis and Edouard Miailhe, who sold it to Jean-Charles Cazes. From Jean-Charles the estate was passed to his son André and then to Jean-Michel Cazes, who also owned Lynch-Bages, and oversaw operations at several AXA-Millésimes properties, including Pichon-Baron and Suduiraut.

At Lynch-Bages Jean-Michel hired Daniel Llose in 1976, and together the two are responsible for that estate's renaissance which continued through to modern times. Daniel and the rest of the team also took responsibility at Ormes de Pez, and quality here improved just as it had at the other Cazes estates. In recent years the next generation has grabbed the reins; Jean-Michel's son Jean-Charles in particular has been taking on more and more responsibility for the winemaking at the Cazes properties, including Ormes de Pez.

The wine is firm and robust, a style typical of the commune, and it certainly offers good value. As Bordeaux prices seem to climb ever upwards, those that have to keep their financial feet on the ground will need estates such as this in order to remain in touch with Bordeaux. There is good quality here, often at a good price. We can only hope that this remains the case in years to come. I expect it will.

Château Raymond-Lafon

Best recent vintage: 2011
Also worth a look: 1999

The discovery of hitherto untasted domaines offering value and quality from outside the established hierarchies of the 1855 and similar classifications is surely one of the holy grails for Bordeaux. Many such domaines hail from little-known, long forgotten or just plain overlooked regions, such as Fronsac or the western slopes of the Entre-Deux-Mers. Finding them hidden among the classified châteaux of the best-known left bank appellations is a rare occurrence indeed, especially in Sauternes where much of the action seems to be focused on the premiers crus, with occasional appearances from a handful of châteaux at the deuxième cru level. And yet that is just what we have in Raymond-Lafon; an unsung, unclassified hero of the Sauternes appellation who, for many I imagine, remains unheard of, and for me – until recently at least – untasted.

The estate's absence from the 1855 classification has one very simple explanation; it only came into being in 1850, by the hand of Monsieur Raymond-Lafon himself, and five years was not sufficient for the estate to establish the strong trading history and track record of prices needed by the merchants drawing up the shortlist

in 1855. And so the estate went unclassified, and remains so to this day. The current incumbents are the Meslier family, the château having been acquired by Francine and Pierre Meslier in 1972. By this time it was in a state of disrepair and in need of rescue and so Pierre, originally an agricultural engineer from Montpellier and at that time manager at nearby Yquem, took control of the vineyards and cellars, ultimately retiring from his post at Yquem to concentrate solely on Raymond-Lafon. Meanwhile Francine took over the management of the château.

After many years the estate has been revitalised and it is now turning out wines to challenge even the very best of the Sauternes 1855 hierarchy. Today the next generation – Marie-Françoise, Charles-Henri and Jean-Pierre – are in charge, having taken over from their parents in 1990. The reputation of the estate under their direction continues to be in the ascendant, the trio winning not just customers but also much good publicity from releasing their highly-rated 2009 at a very favourable price, a noteworthy act in what was otherwise a highly hyped and highly priced vintage. Raymond-Lafon is producing at a very high level, I believe: certainly deuxième cru, and in fact I wouldn't argue with anyone placing it one step above that, even. These are utterly delicious wines.

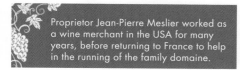

Proprietor Jean-Pierre Meslier worked as a wine merchant in the USA for many years, before returning to France to help in the running of the family domaine.

Château Doisy-Védrines

The three Doisy vineyards of Barsac – Doisy-Daëne, Doisy-Védrines and Doisy-Dubroca – were all created by the division of a single estate, the origins of which are not well documented.

Best recent vintage: 2011
Also worth a look: 2007

T he earliest records relating to the Doisy vineyard are from the 18th century, and describe an estate to the south of Château Coutet owned by the Védrines family. The newlyweds Jean Védrines and Marie Raymond settled in a little village here named La Pinesse, which was owned by the Raymonds. Here they established an estate complete with château, and they, or their immediate descendents, are likely to have been responsible for the planting of vines. Within the same century they were expanding their domaine, acquiring a small portion of the Coutet vineyard when it was sold off following the execution (by guillotine) of its owner, Gabriel-Barthélémy-Romain de Filhot, in 1794.

By the early 19th century the estate was recognised as one of the leading vineyards of Barsac, although it was about this time (the exact date isn't clear, sadly) the Doisy vineyard was divided. The largest part remained with the original owners, the Védrines family, and it was this part that was the origin of what is today Doisy-Védrines. The Védrines family remained at the estate until the middle of the 19th century, until in 1851 they sold out to the Boireau family, and it has remained

with their descendents through to modern day. It passed first to a Madame Teyssonneau who ran the estate well into her dotage, eventually bequeathing the estate at the age of 94. It then came to her grandson, Pierre Castéja, who ran the estate during the remainder of the 20th century. With his passing Doisy-Védrines came to the next generation of the Castéja family, Olivier.

Inevitably the three Doisy vineyards invite comparison, particularly Doisy-Daëne and Doisy-Védrines which both have a higher profile than Doisy-Dubroca. On the one or two occasions I have tasted them against one another, of the same vintage, I note that I have decided slightly in favour of Doisy-Védrines, but this comes down to no more than personal taste, I'm sure. Nevertheless, whether your preference is Doisy-Daëne or Doisy-Védrines, there is no doubt that there is both quality and value in abundance to be found here.

8

Top 10 To Try

When it comes to the wine, quality at any particular château can wax and wane. Change can come for many reasons; new blood in the shape of a new owner, investment from a big-business proprietor, or even the arrival of a new vineyard manager. The following profiles highlight ten châteaux where the past few vintages have seen significant developments such as these, and most importantly an accompanying improvement in the quality of the wines.

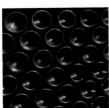

Château
Brane-Cantenac

Best recent vintage: **2009**
Also worth a look: **2005**

The history of Brane-Cantenac can be traced as far back as the early 18th century, when it was owned by the Gorce family, and was known as Château Gorce (and for a while as Château Gorce-Guy). The family had acquired the estate probably around 1735, and were clearly active in the area of viticulture; the vineyard expanded, and the price of the wine rose steadily towards the end of the century, a sure sign that Brane-Cantenac was recognised as a source of good quality. It was Baron Hector de Brane, acquiring the property in 1833, who renamed the estate Brane-Cantenac, and this was the name under which the property was classified in 1855. Under Baron Hector's tenure the vineyard continued to expand and production increased even further. The château, at that time a small construction dating from the 17th century, remained largely untouched.

The estate came into the hands of the current proprietors, the Lurton family, in 1925. Lucien Lurton worked hard to improve the situation at Brane-Cantenac, as has his son Henri, who began

working at the estate in 1986, taking full control in 1992. Today he remains in charge, although it is technical director Christophe Capdeville who runs the vineyard and cellar.

Brane-Cantenac has been something of a slumbering giant, a large estate situated near the top of the 1855 classification – ranked as a second growth – and yet I was never enamoured of the wines. Indeed, some have even gone so far as to suggest Brane-Cantenac received a higher classification than was warranted because of the influence of its famous proprietor, the noble Baron Hector. I am aware of no evidence for such allegations, which also ignore Brane-Cantenac's consistently high ranking over several classifications (over many decades). In addition, we have new evidence to suggest that its position is warranted. A tasting of the wines produced over the last decade at this estate, undertaken in October 2011, showed that quality was on the up. And unlike nearby Château Lascombes, another second growth which underperformed for many years, this has not been achieved merely by increasing the concentration and extraction within the wines, and then smothering them in new oak. Rather there is increased focus, elegance, purity and finesse. Under the guiding hands of Capdeville and Lurton these wines are now the epitome of the Margaux appellation.

One small part of Brane-Cantenac's renaissance has been achieved with optical sorting, a relatively new technology in Bordeaux. Individual grapes are optically analysed as they pass along a moving conveyor belt – those the wrong size, or not of adequate colour (and therefore ripeness) are automatically rejected.

Château Gruaud-Larose

Best recent vintage: 2010
Also worth a look: 2009

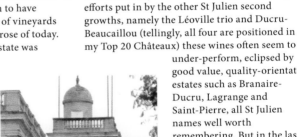

An 18th-century proprietor, the eccentric Chevalier de Gruaud not only built a watch-tower over his vineyards to observe his workers, but would also raise a British, German or other national flag after harvest to indicate who should buy the wine according to its style.

The exact origins of Château Gruaud-Larose are unknown, as direct references to the estate do not appear in the early 18th century. The knight Joseph Stanislas Gruaud is generally credited with the first steps towards its creation but it was two descendents – a priest and a magistrate – who seem to have gathered together the large swathe of vineyards that would become the Gruaud-Larose of today.

During the 19th century the estate was divided, and for over half a century the two halves operated as separate entities, although with the subsequent purchase of both halves by the Cordier group this situation came to an end. The Cordier family held tenure until it was sold in 1983, eventually coming to the current proprietors, the Merlaut family, in 1997. Having said that, based on my experiences tasting older vintages from the 1980s and beyond, the last two decades are not representative of what this estate is capable of. Although there was a flurry of excitement with the 2000 vintage, when the wine was rich and spicy, with a depth and layered concentration that was befitting of a highly ranked second growth property (and more than a

handful of people likened it to the wine of a first growth), there have been a number of disappointments since.

In many recent vintages the wines of Gruaud-Larose have just not been that exciting; decent wines, yes, but considering the sterling efforts put in by the other St Julien second growths, namely the Léoville trio and Ducru-Beaucaillou (tellingly, all four are positioned in my Top 20 Châteaux) these wines often seem to under-perform, eclipsed by good value, quality-orientated estates such as Branaire-Ducru, Lagrange and Saint-Pierre, all St Julien names well worth remembering. But in the last year or two I sense a renewed vigour in the wines of Gruaud-Larose. They remain distinctive, elegant too, but there are more layers to them than we're used to. Both the 2010 and 2009 were at least worthy of the estate's ranking, and that is more than can be said of most other recent vintages, save perhaps the 2000. Of course, these two vintages were very good across the whole of Bordeaux, so I'm looking forward to reassessing future vintages of Gruaud-Larose, and I'm full of optimism for them.

Château Lafon-Rochet

For the 2000 vintage the Tesseron family rebranded Lafon-Rochet, changing from a restrained cream coloured label to a rich yellow-gold, with capsules to match. And the château was painted the same colour; it has weathered a little over the years, and these days makes for an appealing sight.

Best recent vintage: 2009
Also worth a look: 2005

T he origins of Lafon-Rochet date back to the 16th century, and it takes its name from Etienne de Lafon, a local parliamentarian who married into the family that owned the estate. When his wife died he retained only a small portion of this property, the rest returning to her family. It was the part he kept that became the Lafon-Rochet we know today, and it was Etienne that bears most responsibility for establishing the vineyard. His descendents inherited the property, it passing through the hands of numerous individuals, until it was eventually acquired by Frederic Audon in the late 19th century.

Following many years of deterioration during the 20th century the property was purchased by Guy Tesseron, the son of a Chanterais family who specialised in the production, blending and selling of Cognac. His acquisition of Lafon-Rochet brought him some untidy vineyards and a collection of derelict buildings. Remarkably, the latter he dealt with by demolition, replacing it with a newly constructed edifice in the 18th-century chartreuse style. In 1975 he also acquired Pontet-Canet. Both châteaux subsequently passed to the next generation with Lafon-Rochet coming to Michel Tesseron.

It was in 2007 that the next transfer of responsibility occurred. Following a disagreement as the harvest loomed the technical director handed in his notice – accompanied by a few choice words, I am told – and the estate was left rudderless. Michel was just about to leave France, and so he telephoned his son Basile, who had long expressed an interest in running the château. The message was simple; Basile could now run the property, the only problems being the technical advisor had just thrown in the towel and the grapes needed picking…soon. Over to you, son! It was a baptism of fire for young Basile, but in a very difficult vintage he seems to have pulled out all the stops. The 2007 from Lafon-Rochet is, provided you take this comment in the context of a fairly mediocre vintage, one of the better wines of the year.

Since then Basile has excelled, helped of course by a decent vintage in 2008, and superlative years with 2009 and 2010. These are very good wines indeed from Lafon-Rochet, and Basile has more than proved himself. He has overseen the construction of a tasting room at the rear of the property which has a superb view over the vines, and he has great plans for the reconstruction and reorganisation of the vineyard in the coming years. I'm sure I'm right in saying there are good times ahead for Lafon-Rochet!

Château La Conseillante

Best recent vintage: 2009
Also worth a look: 2008

This estate appears to owe its name to Catherine Conseillan, a metal dealer based in Libourne who established the vineyard close to the border between the communes of Pomerol and St Emilion midway through the 18th century. The property came to the Leperche-Princeteau family during the 1840s, before it was acquired by Louis Nicolas in 1871. It is from this point that we may trace a direct line through to the owners of today, who are his descendents. In current times it is Bertrand Nicolas and Marie-France Nicolas d'Arfeuille who run the estate, assisted by manager Jean-Michel Laporte, who must certainly be credited with a large part of the improvements in the wine at La Conseillante in recent years.

It is Jean-Michel who I think of as the 'new blood' at La Conseillante. Although he joined the team in 2001, which means he now has ten vintages under his belt, his contribution to La Conseillante's current position in the Pomerol hierarchy is so significant that I cannot help but draw attention to him in this guide, even if ten years is stretching the definition of 'new blood' somewhat. The terroir here has always been

capable of producing great wine, as a taste of the 1945 and 1990 vintages, both sampled early in 2011, told me. But Jean-Michel has pushed the envelope a little more I think, and as a consequence recent vintages of La Conseillante have done nothing but impress this particular palate. His innovations have been plentiful, including adopting a more hands-off approach in the winery, as well as introducing a second wine, newly created with the 2007 vintage, named Duo de Conseillante. This takes the fruit from a patch of vines on more sandy soils near Cheval Blanc, thus saving the pick of the crop for the grand vin itself.

Perhaps most tellingly it is not the great vintages, such as 2009 and 2010 (or looking further back 1982 or 1990), but the weaker years (such as 2007) in which La Conseillante has proved its quality. As always, the ability to turn out such an admirable wine in such a weak and wet vintage is the hallmark of a great estate. If there is any recent vintage that really shows what the vines here are capable of, however, it is 2008; this is a superb wine for the vintage, and is one of the best wines from the commune, I think. Unfortunately, the cat is long since out of the bag on the quality to be found here today, and prices have risen accordingly.

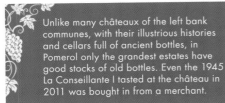

Unlike many châteaux of the left bank communes, with their illustrious histories and cellars full of ancient bottles, in Pomerol only the grandest estates have good stocks of old bottles. Even the 1945 La Conseillante I tasted at the château in 2011 was bought in from a merchant.

Château Labégorce

Best recent vintage: **2010**
Also worth a look: **2009**

The origins of Labégorce lie with the Gorce (or Gorsse) family, perhaps as far back as the 14th century. The family were originally merchants, gradually climbing the social ladder in Bordeaux, assuming a more aristocratic standing in the community as they did so. This did them no good during the Revolution, sadly, when, like so many other estates in Bordeaux, Labégorce was confiscated as a bien national, a national asset to be divided up and sold off. Doing so gave rise to three estates that maintained their existence as independent properties through to the early years of the 21st century, before they were unified under the name of Labégorce once more.

The man who wanted to reunify the estate was Hubert Perrodo, a wealthy French industrialist who made his fortune in the petrochemical industry. Perrodo was on a polo-playing trip to Bordeaux in 1989 when he learned that Labégorce was for sale. He visited the estate and bought it, adding nearby L'Abbé Gorsse de Gorsse – one of the other parts of the original estate – in 2002. Unfortunately, the vineyards had already been bought by Château Margaux in a little publicised

acquisition, but the buildings – although not the original Labégorce château, which was burnt to the ground in 1965 – were his. Then, in 2005, he purchased Labégorce-Zédé from Luc Thienpont; with most of the vineyard and all of the original buildings in his possession, the unification of Labégorce was complete. How tragic then, that having achieved his goal, Hubert Perrodo never lived to see it all come together; he was killed in a hiking accident in Courchevel late in 2006.

Nobody would have been surprised if the Perrodo family, bereft with grief, had sold off their father's estates. But Hubert's daughter, Nathalie Perrodo, proved her mettle when she stepped up to the mark, and began to manage the Labégorce vineyards. The reunification went ahead, although it was not until the 2010 vintage that the wine represented the newly recreated Labégorce estate.

Being blunt, the wines of Labégorce have until recently never truly excited my palate. I know the estate has its fans, many of whom cite the 1996 vintage as a shining example of what the estate (or at least one part of the now unified estate) is capable of. My own experiences have been less thrilling. Having said that, there is new direction now that Nathalie is at the helm, bringing a sense of invigoration to Château Labégorce. This seems to be coming through in the wine, and the incorporation of better-quality fruit from the Labégorce-Zédé vineyards is perhaps the reason why. Certainly, the 2010 Labégorce was one of the most convincing vintages from this estate that I have tasted. The 2009 was equally good, and I looking forward to seeing what happens in the future.

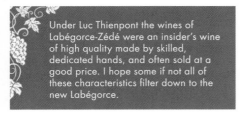

Under Luc Thienpont the wines of Labégorce-Zédé were an insider's wine of high quality made by skilled, dedicated hands, and often sold at a good price. I hope some if not all of these characteristics filter down to the new Labégorce.

Château Petit Village

There doesn't seem to be a very convincing explanation for the name Petit Village; it has been said that the name refers to the appearance of the estate from afar, which was such that the cluster of buildings resembled a small village.

51

Best recent vintage: 2011
Also worth a look: 2005

The origins of this estate are distant and not easy to distinguish. There were vines here during the 18th century, although identifying the owner at this time is no easy task. It is not until it is purchased by Fernand Ginestet in 1919, shortly after the close of World War I, that a definite history of Petit Village becomes available. The Ginestet family were proprietors here for at least five decades before it came to the Prats family of Cos d'Estournel through marriage, and although they poured money into the property they ultimately sold it to AXA Millésimes. It was the AXA geniuses Jean-Michel Cazes and Daniel Llose that took charge at first, but eventually responsibility fell to Christian Seely, who oversees operations here as he does at Pichon-Baron and Suduiraut. In 2002 a planned sale to Gérard Perse, the ebullient proprietor of Pavie, fell through, and thus Petit Village today remains with AXA.

Although there were already positive signs, it is only in the last few years, really since the property escaped transfer into the hands of Perse, that the wines have demonstrated the greatest improvement. An active program of reinvestment has included: replanting of some Cabernet Franc in 2004 and Merlot in 2005, the renovation of the barrel cellar in the latter of these two years, the construction of a new receiving area for the fruit in

2006 (along with new vats), and a second, completely new barrel cellar in 2007. With such heavy investment it is only natural that we should be looking for significant developments in the quality of the wine.

Published critical ratings of Petit Village are interesting to follow, as there is no unity of opinion, as far as I can tell. Some admire the wines; others see them as dull and uninspiring. I think I am somewhere in the middle, but certainly closer to the first position than the second. Tasting recent vintages of Petit Village in their youth, they appear to be full of promise, but where they differ from their peers is in both the flesh and texture. These wines do not exhibit the heady, seductive, fleshy or even flashy style of Pomerol, instead they show a much more restrained character, opening up a little with a few years of bottle age. They offer an attractive style but nevertheless I would be the first to agree that we are not, judging by recent vintages, looking at the top tier of the Pomerol appellation here. Yet, I know the AXA team are continuing to work hard, meaning this is certainly an estate to watch.

© Château Petit-Village 2008 photo A.Benoit - deepix

Château La Pointe

Few estates in Pomerol are graced by so grand a château as that found at La Pointe, especially when we remember that it is blessed by several hectares of formal gardens, including a collection of trees many centuries old.

Best recent vintage: 2010
Also worth a look: 2009

A s is often the case in Pomerol, the history of Château La Pointe is rather sketchy. What we do know is that the Chaperon family were early proprietors, and that they built the grand château. In 1941 the d'Arfeuille family acquired the estate, and they held tenure here until selling in 2007 to Generali France, one of France's leading insurance providers, who were perhaps keen to follow AXA into the world of Bordeaux. The group already owned a vineyard in northern Italy as well as another Bordeaux estate, Château de France, but La Pointe – with a price tag somewhere between €32 and €35 million – was certainly a step up for them. The deal was struck, and Generali France appointed Eric Monneret, an agricultural engineer who started out with

Raymond-Lafon in Sauternes and who also runs Château La France, a somewhat larger estate at 90 hectares, as managing director.

One of the first moves funded by Generali France was a detailed soil analysis by geologist Pierre Becheler, followed by improvements to the field drainage, carried out during the summer months of 2008 and 2009. Following this there was also some restructuring of the vineyards. In particular this featured a grubbing-up of the Cabernet Sauvignon vines; these once accounted for 15% of the vineyard. What was left was mostly Merlot, now accounting for 85% of the vineyard, and 15% Cabernet Franc. Some environmentally friendly initiatives were also introduced during this reinvigoration of the property, including a water recuperation system (evidence of which is the large water storage tank just outside the cellars) and solar energy equipment. The percentage of new oak used for ageing the wine has also been increased. Perhaps most importantly, in January 2008 Generali France engaged the services of Hubert de Boüard de Laforest, a man perhaps best known for his work at Angélus and increasingly Bellevue in St Emilion, but who consults widely, with a particular emphasis on the right bank appellations.

And as for the wines, it is perhaps too soon to judge, but there are clear signs of rebirth here. I look forward to seeing how these developments at La Pointe pan out in the coming years. I think the results might be very good indeed.

Château Fourcas Hosten

Best recent vintage: **2005**
Also worth a look: **2006**

T he story of Fourcas Hosten harks back to the days of the Hosten family, proprietors in the 18th and early 19th centuries. In modern times, however, this estate has been in the ownership of an American syndicate, led by Peter Sichel, who purchased the property in 1971. The ranks of the new owners subsequently swelled with the addition of some French merchants and local proprietors, creating a strong multinational board. This French-American consortium built the estate a solid reputation, until 2006 when, in an announcement that surprised the industry, it was revealed that Fourcas-Hosten had been sold.

The new owners were brothers Laurent and Renaud Momméja, names perhaps unfamiliar to wine savants, but to dedicated followers of fashion they will be instantly recognisable; the Momméja family is behind one of the fashion world's most famous labels, Hermès. Ebullient and enthusiastic, the new owners announced that they had fallen in love with "this beautiful property and its great wine". What they have acquired is not just an admirable Médoc vineyard, more than half of which is characterised by valuable gravel-rich terroir, but also an attractive chartreuse-style

Château Fourcas Hosten is situated in Listrac, a small commune located between the more famous left-bank appellations of St Julien and Margaux. These 'lesser' regions are often overlooked but can be a source of great value wines.

château situated at the heart of a 3-hectare park. Naturally, though, there has been some improvement and investment; there were extensive works in 2008, including a renovation of the three cellars and château, new equipment and barrels, and some tidying up in the vineyard. The vineyards and winemaking are overseen by manager Patrice Pagès, who was retained by the Mommejas following their purchase, with assistance from oenologist Eric Boissenot.

Tasting these wines it seems clear to me that Fourcas Hosten is indeed a source of good value Bordeaux – a rarely encountered beast. No, it is not the unsung equivalent of Léoville Las-Cases or Vieux Château Certan, but it is a source of nicely fashioned wines, restrained and dry rather than sweet and rich, food-friendly and savoury. Just the sort of wines, in fact, that so many lament cannot be found in Bordeaux today. I hope that this trend continues under the new management – and that the significant investment so far put in place yields good results.

Château
La Vieille Cure

Best recent vintage: **2005**
Also worth a look: **2008**

The wines of Fronsac were at one time in great demand in the French court, but that was during the appellation's 18th-century heyday. With the arrival of phylloxera and the devastation of France's vineyards, Fronsac was one of a number of regions that started a slow spiral into decline. The region has seen hard times as the appellation has faded into the shadow of the grand estates of nearby Pomerol and St Emilion. Fortunately, outside investors have helped a number of these forlorn properties to regain some of their former glory, and Château La Vieille Cure is one such estate.

It was in 1986 that Americans Colin Ferenbach and Peter Sachs provided the necessary financial boost to Château La Vieille Cure. With this fresh investment of funds there came the introduction of lower yields, greater selection at harvest time, new oak barrels and new equipment in the cellars. More recently the method of harvesting itself has come under scrutiny, and as a result there have been some changes made to this process, including harvesting into small plastic trays in a bid to avoid damaging the fragile grapes

before they reach the fermentation area. Here the fruit is now destemmed and then passed over a sorting table where eight workers pick out unwanted material.

The end result of these new processes has been a consistent increase in the quality and approachability of the wines on offer. And it comes as no surprise, therefore, to learn that the château has rediscovered commercial success, with exports to over 20 countries worldwide – led by the UK and the USA – and good sales on the home market as well. The wines, which are certainly built for short-term cellaring, although perhaps that is changing, remain good value, and while Fronsac remains under-appreciated I suspect this situation will persist.

Fronsac and Canon-Fronsac can make a happy hunting ground for the bargain-hungry. Watch out also for Château de la Rivière, Château Fontenil (home to the famous international winemaking consultant Michel Rolland), Château Haut-Carles and Château Moulin Haut Laroque.

Château Hosanna

The name Hosanna has ecumenical overtones, not unusual in this appellation; many of the top estates of Pomerol are gathered around the village church, and Hosanna is no exception.

Best recent vintage: 2009
Also worth a look: 2008

T he story of Hosanna, a property in Pomerol for many years known as Certan-Marzelle and then Certan-Giraud, begins with the Sertan estate of the late-18th century. Sertan, or Certan, was a property in the hands of the Demay family, wealthy landowners and négociants who originated from Scotland. During the 19th century small parcels of the estate were sold off, including one which became Certan-Marzelle before being rechristened Certan-Giraud by new proprietors, the Giraud family, in 1956.

The wines of the Giraud era, particularly during the immediate decades prior to 1999, were not the best the estate has produced. It was perhaps no surprise that the estate was sold, Certan-Giraud having been acquired at this time by the Moueix family in a joint purchase with the Delon family, the latter known for their successful tenure of Léoville-Las-Cases. The property was divided, giving the Delons another 4 hectares – a portion of the estate called the Clos du Roy – to incorporate into their new Pomerol domaine, Château Nenin, whilst Christian Moueix took what remained.

It was Christian's intention to rename what came to him simply Certan, removing the Giraud appendage as per the wishes of the vendors, but being a prudent businessman he first called upon the proprietors of similarly named Pomerol estates, including Vieux

Château Certan and Certan de May, to ascertain whether this would be viewed as an infringement. There were no objections from Alexandre Thienpont at the former, but at the latter Madame Barreau-Bader was not content. The only solution would be a completely new name, and thus Château Hosanna was born. As well as the 4 hectares taken by the Delon family another 2 hectares of purely Merlot were cleaved off to recreate Château Certan-Marzelle, the name an acknowledgement of the proprietors prior to the Giraud era. What was left for Hosanna amounted to not quite 4.5 hectares. Moueix thus added two distinct properties to his portfolio.

When tasting Hosanna under the auspices of Christian Moueix in his quayside offices in Libourne, the wine tends to be offered for tasting towards the end of the line-up, an indication of how the Moueix clan see this wine within their portfolio. I generally find the wines of Hosanna to be successful, albeit in a rich and substantial style. The 2008 was perhaps a step up, providing fabulous clarity and polish, with a seamless texture alongside the substance. But in 2009 and 2010 the wines are excellent, and it seems to me we have another high quality player on the Pomerol field here.

Your FREE copy of THE WEEK magazine

You may well have heard about *The Week*, but if you've never seen the magazine, why not allow us to **send you a copy absolutely FREE?**

The Week is a joy to read, distilling **the best of British and international media** into a succinct digest. It will keep you entertained as well as informed. See for yourself how you can stay up to date with **the most important stories, views and opinions in news and politics from the past 7 days.**

Time is precious. If you've found yourself getting swamped with information overload, it's time you tried *The Week*. Once you start reading the magazine, you'll wonder how you ever managed without it.

FOR YOUR **FREE** COPY CALL **0808 1783 970 NOW**

Call freephone 0808 1783 970 to request your FREE copy and quote 'Wine'.

9

Understanding Bordeaux

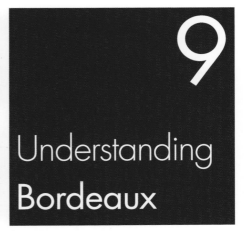

Knowing the different regions of Bordeaux is essential (as we shall see in the next chapter), but it is not everything. In this chapter I give a run-down of some of the other features that make Bordeaux what it is. This includes everything from grape varieties, climate, viticulture and my take on modern winemaking, through to the second and third wines of Bordeaux and some background information on the peculiar way in which Bordeaux wine is bought and sold.

Bordeaux Varieties

Almost all red Bordeaux wines are blends, so it is usually a matter of which variety dominates – almost always Cabernet Sauvignon or Merlot in the case of red wines – rather than wines which are 100% one variety or another. Only a few wines are what we might call 'monovarietal', such as the 100% Merlot Le Pin, or the very rare example of a left bank wine that is 100% Cabernet Sauvignon, such as 1961 Lafite-Rothschild.

Cabernet Sauvignon: This variety is renowned for the wines it produces on the well-drained, gravelly soils on the left bank of the Gironde. It is usually blended with other components, principally Merlot, but there are a number of other eligible varieties.

Merlot: This variety is most famous for the wines from the right bank, especially from Pomerol and St Emilion. The blended variety is classically Cabernet Franc rather than Cabernet Sauvignon, although both can be found. Outside the classic left bank communes of St Julien, Pauillac and so on, Merlot may also dominate. Because of this versatility (and perhaps because it ripens early), Merlot is today the most widely planted variety in Bordeaux, accounting for as much as 63% of the entire vineyard.

Blending Varieties: These are led by Cabernet Franc which plays a major role in a handful of wines, such as Cheval Blanc where it is the principal variety, and it contributes a significant percentage to many right bank wines, less so on the left bank. It brings perfume, spice and freshness. Petit Verdot gives a deeply coloured and tannic wine useful for bringing substance and structure to a blend. Malbec, best associated with the wines of Cahors, is also eligible but less commonly encountered than the first two

blenders. There are also small plantings of Carmenère here and there (and other varieties), such as the experimental plot that can be found at Brane-Cantenac.

The shortlist of white varieties also has two star players, and again most wines are blends, sweeter wines usually more dependent on Semillon, whereas drier wines will often feature more Sauvignon Blanc.

Semillon: This was once the most widely planted variety in Bordeaux, before the red wines came to dominate. Its thin skin leaves it susceptible to botrytis rot, essential for the production of Sauternes. Although occasionally it may appear alone, such as at Château Climens, it is usually blended with Sauvignon Blanc.

Sauvignon Blanc: As well as a blending partner in Sauternes, and occasionally the dominant variety (such as in Château Doisy-Daëne's super cuvée, L'Extravagant de Doisy-Daëne), it plays an important role in the dry white wines of Graves and the Entre-Deux-Mers.

Blending Varieties: First place goes to Muscadelle, a difficult variety to work with, occasionally blended into Sauternes, but rarely more than a few percent. Secondly there is Sauvignon Gris, an easy variety to forget. It may be found in the Graves region with the Sauvignon Blanc, and also in Château Monbousquet's Bordeaux Blanc. Occasional plots of Ugni Blanc and Colombard may be found, but are of no real importance.

Bordeaux's Climate

Bordeaux has a temperate climate thanks to the moderating influence of the Atlantic Ocean, an effect which reaches far inland thanks to the presence of the Gironde Estuary. The winter is generally mild and rarely generates the sort of temperatures that are severe enough to permanently damage the vines, although this has not always been so. The 1956 vintage is a case in point; a severe winter frost killed many vines resulting in a widespread need for replanting in following years.

Spring and autumn are also usually mild, although spring frosts can also cause severe problems, damaging the tender new buds, shoots and leaves. Again, this is now becoming something of a historical issue, it seems (although that does not stop the Bordelais worrying about it). The most recent spring frost to do any great damage was in April 1991. The thermometers bottomed out well below freezing, and sunk as low as -7C on Sunday April 21st. It was described by Christian Moueix as "a disaster"; the fact that many still remember the exact date, now 20 years on, gives some indication of just how much of a disaster it was. In these days of ever-rising global temperatures, when practically every other vintage coming out of Bordeaux is a Vintage of the Century, it seems difficult to even conceive of such a catastrophic event, but in some areas the frost wiped out "between 80% and 100% of the crop", according to Moueix. And because the replacement buds had a late start, what was harvested was picked late, under an autumnal deluge. The wines were, in many cases, the worst to come out of Bordeaux in many decades.

In recent years we have seen that the summertime temperatures in Bordeaux can climb very high, with the earliest harvest on record (and French documents record many centuries of data) being in 2003, although some estates report picking even earlier in 2011. The more recent 2009 vintage was also characterised by warm and dry weather, although the effect on the wines seems slightly more tempered than it was in 2003. And, on the other hand, weather patterns are increasingly unpredictable. The 2011 vintage is the perfect example, with a hot spring and a cool summer, a sort of 'year in reverse'. Summer hail and storms are not uncommon and can devastate vineyards, stripping the vines of leaves and fruit.

Naturally this leads us to climate change. There is no doubt that the style of wines coming out of Bordeaux has changed much in the last few decades. Partly this is due to new understanding of the vineyards and winemaking, but it is also down to climate change and altered fruit ripening. Grapes are sweeter and in general the wines have more slick fruit and more alcohol than they used to. The variety to suffer most is Merlot which ripens early – the 2003 and 2009 vintages saw some plots of Merlot in Bordeaux exceed 15% alcohol.

Organics and Biodynamics

There are many facets to good vineyard management; how densely should the vines be planted, and how high should they be trained? Opinion on both has changed much in Bordeaux in the past decades. Which rootstocks to choose (almost all vines in France are grafts, French scions grafted onto American rootstocks, the only guaranteed protection against phylloxera)? Do you want to work the soil with plough and hoe, tractor or horse, or would you rather plant grass between the rows of vines and then leave well alone? To cover all methods is beyond the scope of this guide, but a few words on the slow shift within Bordeaux from a viticulture reliant on chemicals towards organic practices are worthwhile.

Bordeaux has had its fair share of vine disease. The 19th century saw the vineyards devastated, largely by pests imported from America on vine cuttings. Phylloxera I have already alluded to, but downy mildew and oidium (also known as powdery mildew), both fungal diseases, have also wreaked havoc. Although chemical treatments failed with phylloxera, they were effective here, with powdered sulphur for oidium and copper (also known as 'Bordeaux mixture') for downy mildew. The humid environment in Bordeaux means both above diseases still thrive today, as does botrytis rot (essential for Sauternes, but undesirable when it comes to red wines). Vine diseases such as eutypiose, esca and black dead arm also take their toll.

All these mean that the adoption of organic viticulture – and throwing chemical treatments (although note that sulphur and copper are permitted within organics) out the door – is not done lightly. The damp climate is often

A memorial to Ernest David and Alexis Millardet, who pioneered the treatment of downy mildew with copper at Dauzac.

touted as a reason organics or biodynamics "won't work" in Bordeaux, but the fact that they both thrive in the more northerly Loire Valley, and that a handful of Bordeaux estates have succeeded with them, suggests there may be another reason organic is being shunned. Chemical viticulture is safe, whereas going organic means taking risk, and big business is risk averse. Loss of the harvest through unchecked disease would mean total loss of income for the year – essentially unthinkable. More enticing is lutte raisonnée, a system of reasoned viticulture which minimises, but doesn't forbid, chemical treatment.

Increasingly aware of the importance of soil health, some estates are embracing organics and biodynamics; there are only a few complete converts to the latter, but a number of estates have been experimenting with both on small plots of land. What validity these experiments and their results have when these plots are surrounded by chemically treated vines, is debatable.

Winemaking the Traditional Way

T he process of winemaking is superficially simple; the fermentation of the sugars in harvested grapes produces alcohol, as well as a wealth of more complex flavours. But even the briefest of closer inspections reveals that this is a multifaceted process, with many decisions and potentially disastrous pitfalls along the way.

Winemaking starts in the vineyard, and every vineyard manager should be aiming to produce the highest quality fruit. Once picked – by hand at the top estates, and this is mandatory for Sauternes which is picked grape by grape – the grapes are sorted in order to exclude leaves, twigs and other non-grape matter, and also to select only perfect, ripe, undamaged fruit. White grapes would then be pressed and the juice transferred into a vat for fermentation, whereas red grapes would be lightly crushed and the juice, skins, pulp and pips fermented together. This is a necessary part of the process, as it is the skin and pips that impart the colour and tannin to the red wine. The transfer is likely to be achieved by pipe, either pumped or with the help of gravity.

Fermentation was traditionally carried out in large oak vats, which were in use for decades, but their downsides were many. They were difficult to clean and thus possibly harboured spoilage

bacteria, and the temperature of the fermenting wine was difficult to control. It wasn't unknown for dry ice to be thrown into the vat when the temperature rose too high during fermentation. These days steel is the most commonly encountered material, although wood still exists, and cement is also making a comeback. Steel brings easy temperature control, whereas cement has a high thermal inertia, so both have benefits.

Thereafter the wine goes into oak barrel for a period of time. Traditionally the red wines will be run off the lees, the sediment of dead yeast cells and other solids, every three months. The dry white wines are more likely to see some lees stirring, otherwise known as bâtonnage, a process which brings a greater depth to the palate (some do this with red as well). Sauternes, meanwhile, will often see out both fermentation and ageing in barrel; yields for Sauternes are much lower, and the small size of these vessels allows for finer control and true plot-by-plot fermentation.

Winemaking tends to be overseen by the technical director, or the régisseur as he may be known. Increasingly outside advice is sought, usually from some of the big name consultants. These might bring a few words of advice, but are just as likely to remind the régisseur of the wealth of technologies that are now available to the 21st-century winemaker.

TOP CONSULTANTS

Quality may be improved, but it can be said that consultants often stamp their own style on a wine. Whether that is good or bad depends on your taste preferences. Top consultants include:
- Jacques & Eric Boissenot
- Michel Rolland
- Stéphane Derenoncourt
- Denis Dubourdieu
- Gilles Pauquet

Winemaking the Modern Way

The modern winemaker has many new tools at his or her fingertips. Some are beneficial, whereas the effects of other technologies are more questionable. Some are perhaps open to abuse, and their use may make wines worse rather than better. Many of the techniques used are likely to influence not only the quality, but also the style of wine – not necessarily a good thing.

An improved understanding of the vineyards might come from geological surveys, possibly using aerial or even satellite data, but the main use of modern machinery in the vineyard is in the shape of the mechanical harvester. Although a vital tool for lesser vineyards where the wines do not command a high price (having an entire team of pickers harvesting by hand is expensive) they are not generally used by the leading châteaux. This is because concerns about damaging the fruit during harvest remain. The only notable proponents of the technique at the cru classé level are the Quié family, proprietors of Croizet-Bages and Rauzan-Gassies.

Perhaps the most notable advance in Bordeaux in recent years concerns fruit selection. Sorting tables came first, allowing inspection of the harvested fruit by eye, and rejection of any substandard material. The technology has been developed and modified, starting with perforated sorting tables which would encourage, through vibration, small low-quality grapes to fall through

the holes. Add-on technologies include sorting by density; the grapes can be floated in grape juice of known concentration, thus allowing separation of those that are ripe (the sugar-heavy grapes sink) from those that are not (as they float). Some sorting techniques also allow for automatic separation of damaged fruit from intact fruit, although this is more important in machine-harvested vineyards.

Optical sorting is the latest craze in Bordeaux; the grapes are passed over a conveyor belt and examined by camera, the data (colour and size) informing as to which grapes are to be retained and which are to be rejected. This technique only appeared in the 2008 vintage, but seemed to be everywhere when I was in Bordeaux just after the 2011 harvest (early October), with these machines visible at half of the properties I visited.

These technologies surely enhance fruit quality, but other later technologies are perhaps more questionable. Yeast inoculation in order to kick-start the fermentation, in a region that has many centuries of winemaking history, hardly seems necessary. Micro-oxygenation, the process of bubbling oxygen through the fermenting wine seems less than natural, although it can have beneficial effects on the wine's texture and flavour. Perhaps most concerning of all is reverse osmosis, a technology used somewhat furtively, its aim being to concentrate the grape juice simply by removing water. Of course, it concentrates all those flavours present...including the nasty ones.

SORTING TECHNIQUES

- Static sorting table
- Vibrating perforated sorting table
- Sorting by density
- Sorting by stickiness/damaged
- Optical sorting

Second and Third Wines

A knock-on effect of sorting is that you end up with rejected fruit on your hands. Clearly some is good for nothing other than composting; no right-minded winemaker would consider doing anything else with grapes that were small, shot or just plain unripe. But what if you had been very strict in your sorting and selection, and you ended up with fruit, and even barrels of wine in your cellar, that were of a good standard, but perhaps not of the supreme level of quality required for your château's premier wine? The answer is to make a second wine, and then offer it at a lower price. Everybody wins; buyers of the first wine have improved quality; buyers of the second wine get a taste of the estate's produce, albeit not the best example, but at a significantly reduced cost; and the proprietor makes the most of his fruit.

Of course second wines have been around much longer than the modern technologies which

have taken fruit selection to a new level. Vineyard managers have long recognised that certain plots always produce the highest quality fruit, year-in and year-out. By contrast, some plots have a lesser character, and the wine is consistently less impressive. It was the fruit of these latter plots, selected by taste, which formed the basis of the second wine. The soils of the plots in question often had much to do with it, the more gravelly vineyards with the best aspect giving the best wines, those that were sandy or which sloped away from the sun destined for the second wine. The fruit of young vines is also usually channelled into the second wine.

For many years second wines offered a good-value opportunity to experience the wine of a famous château at a bargain price. Sadly today this is not so true; the prices of many have climbed considerably, led by Carruades de Lafite, the second wine of Lafite-Rothschild, the price driven skywards by Asian demand. Some second wines now command prices higher than an entire case of wine from other châteaux, and in most cases these wines just aren't worth that sort of money. This remains true even though many châteaux are working increasingly hard on ameliorating the quality of their second wine, channelling lower-quality fruit into a third wine, or selling it off in bulk.

TEN SECOND WINES WORTH KNOWING

- Pavillon Rouge du Château Margaux (Château Margaux)
- La Petite Église (Château Église-Clinet)
- La Chapelle d'Ausone (Château Ausone)
- Le Petit Cheval (Château Cheval Blanc)
- Les Forts de Latour (Château Latour)
- Carruades de Lafite (Château Lafite-Rothschild)
- Clarence de Haut-Brion (Châteaux Haut-Brion & La Mission Haut-Brion)
- Le Petit Mouton (Château Mouton-Rothschild)
- Pensées de Lafleur (Château Lafleur)
- Les Tourelles de Longueville (Château Pichon-Baron)

The Peculiar Market

O nce the wine is finished, it has to be sold. The system by which this is achieved in Bordeaux is very peculiar; a thorough examination deserves a book all of its own, but I've pulled together some of the more weird and wonderful elements here.

The Courtiers

Big Bordeaux châteaux might be owned by insurance companies and supermarket magnates these days, but they were once homes to noble families. The superior attitude of the Bordeaux nobility was such that they refused to deal with the chattering merchant classes, the very men who would pay them for the wine that came from their estate. And thus the void between them was filled by the courtier, who would buy from the proprietors and then pass the wine onto the merchants (the négociants), taking a cut (typically 2% – enough to develop some serious wealth) along the way. The courtier still exists in Bordeaux today, although there are only a handful working with the top châteaux, among about 120 who serve the needs of the entire region.

The Négociants

The négociants acquired their wines from the courtiers, and during the 19th century their role was not only to take and ship the wine, but a little judicious blending was also par for the course. The wines from Hermitage in the Rhône Valley were a popular and respected addition, a practice openly declared on the wine lists of the day. This the négociants did in their cellars which today still line the quayside in Bordeaux. Historically they made their fortunes in this way, typically taking a 10-15% slice of the action. Today there are 400-or-so négociants still very active in Bordeaux, often soaking up huge volumes of stock from the châteaux. In modern times their role is more one of trading, marketing and developing foreign markets; their blending activities are a thing of the past!

The Place and En Primeur

The négociants need somewhere to sell the wine, and this is the role of the Place de Bordeaux, the local trading place for Bordeaux wine. Here the wine with its new sale price is floated, and buyers can take the wine if the price is right. These buyers might be big name merchants, or perhaps importers who will pass the wine onto retailers in their own country, and these businesses also need to take a percentage. The Place is active all year round, but the activity really picks up with the release of the new vintage during the spring after the harvest. At this point the wine is bought and sold in barrel, a system known as en primeur. It will be delivered to the buyer once bottled, perhaps 18 months later. There is more on en primeur on page 143.

The system of selling wine in Bordeaux is clearly antiquated, and it works to increase the cost of the wine to the final consumer – you and me. But it continues on for one simple reason – it works to the benefit of Bordeaux.

10

Communes & Classifications

Bordeaux is a gigantic wine region, producing more wine each year than Australia in its entirety. Daunting as this may sound, the wines of greatest interest come from only a select number of the region's communes, and just two-hundred-or-so leading châteaux. This guide provides a run-down of the principal wine-producing regions of Bordeaux, as well as some detail on the region's weird and wonderful wine classification systems.

Introduction

T he first time I experienced the bitter cold of a winter in the vineyards, I was in Bordeaux. Never before had I witnessed the rows of bare vines, devoid of their greenery, so stark and lifeless. And never before had I directly experienced the iciness that these vines endure during the darker months of the year. The temperature was certainly not the coldest – I seem to recall the thermometer reading 3C as we left the château – but out in the flat, rather featureless, windswept vineyard it seemed much colder than the mercury would suggest. Within a quarter of an hour my feet were blocks of ice, my hands were completely numb, and I would swear my nose was turning blue.

It was thus remarkable to note that the team working their way through the vineyard pruning the vines had, despite our relatively early start, probably already been at work for several hours. And they were still going strong, helped no doubt by well chosen and more appropriate clothing than my rather thin skiing fleece. And with several vineyards to complete before the sap began to rise, signifying the arrival of spring, they had to keep working at a good pace.

This is a situation repeated all over the world, every year, although particularly in Bordeaux. Being the world's largest wine region, there are approximately 120,000 hectares of vines here. Assuming a planting density of 6,000 vines per hectare (a conservative estimate – some properties will plant at 8,000 or even 10,000 vines per hectare) that makes for at least 720 million vines in Bordeaux alone, all pruned annually, each one by hand.

Having completed numerous visits to Bordeaux, I have gained more experience of the region than any other in France – indeed any other wine region in existence, European or otherwise. It is an area that has seen dramatic winds of change sweep through its vineyards and cellars in the past few decades. Quality has improved across the board, but the style of wine has changed in tandem, a fact some Bordeaux lovers of old lament, and I have a lot of sympathy for their position.

Despite this apparent metamorphosis, there are many facets of the region that remain unchanged, and the traditional birds-eye view of Bordeaux still holds largely true. With the passage of time proprietors and managers will come and go, while oenologists' fees may wax and wane, but some things are seemingly immutable. The regions, regulations and vineyards we have inherited from history, and seem unwilling to change. This part of my guide covers all these aspects of Bordeaux, region-by-region, complete with my hints and tips as to the top châteaux in each case.

During the 20th century Sauternes has seen more than its fair share of dilapidated châteaux and untended vineyards. Low yields are an inherent aspect of grape dehydration through Noble Rot, and low yields result in fewer bottles to sell; thus to commit to making Sauternes is a significant undertaking. With sweet wines increasingly unfashionable, and traditional markets damaged by the wars and depression that dominated the first half of the last century, it is no surprise that so many of the estates lay untouched and seemingly unloved for decades. And for those that kept going, not all was rosy. With no money to invest, barrels were used for vintage after vintage, which naturally affected the quality of the wine. Dirty, infected wood does a wine little good, although avoiding its use altogether may also be detrimental – fermentation and ageing in oak barrel does seem to help in fleshing out Sauternes. Winemaking became heavy-handed in some circumstances, especially in the face of some less than favourable vintages. In many cases sweetness was ensured by chaptalisation, the addition of sugar to the fermenting must, rather than relying on botrytis and grape sugars. Sulphur has also been a problem – a hefty slug will soon bring the fermentation to an end, and the unfermented sugar gives the sweetness. Today, happily, the better estates eschew both these practices.

Perhaps one of the more controversial techniques introduced in the Sauternes region has been cryo-extraction. It was at Château Rayne-Vigneau in the 1980s, under the direction of Jean Merlaut, that the concept of cryo-extraction was first pioneered. Botrytis cinerea requires very specific conditions, and with a damp harvest there is a danger that the shrivelled and sugar-rich berries will turn to grey rot, and that the quality will be reduced or even ruined altogether. This was a particular problem with the 1982 harvest, and Jean Merlaut, together with Professors Chauvet and Sudraud from the University of Bordeaux and the newly installed régisseur Patrick Eymery (of Château Guiraud), agreed to some trials of freezing the berries in order to remove water, leaving only the rich, botrytised juice, thereby potentially eliminating the problem of a wet harvest. Naturally the process has its detractors, who quite rightly point out that concentration in this way will only accentuate the flaws already present in the wine.

Technologies and manipulations accepted, Sauternes remains the world's foremost region for sweet wine. Quality has risen sharply at many estates; the wines can be superb and yet remain under-valued, especially considering the pain-staking work and dedication that goes into producing them every year.

Margaux

There is no doubt that today Château Margaux itself that acts as standard-bearer for this small part of Bordeaux. The wines are superlative and typify what is most exciting about the commune, but this has not always been the case. Although today, under the direction of the Mentzelopoulos family and with Paul Pontallier running the cellars, the estate has been turning out wines worthy of first growth status for several decades, there was a period during the 1970s when the wines were very sorry indeed. And yet Château Margaux was still representative of the appellation, for this is a commune that has long been dogged by the presence of underperforming properties.

Looking through the recent history of the deuxièmes crus during the 20th century only emphasises this point. For example we have the two Rauzan estates, Ségla and Gassies, the first of which has been revitalised with the financial backing of Chanel, although even before the wines were often good, in my opinion. However Gassies has been struggling for years, and although there have been murmurings of a recovery, I've yet to

see any sign of one. Durfort-Vivens is perhaps in the same position, and some would levy similar criticism at Brane-Cantenac, although some recent vintages have been pretty impressive. Lascombes is perhaps even more controversial than all of the above combined; for many years a source of dismal wines, the estate was born again under the aegis of Alain Reynaud and Michel Rolland, with appropriate financial backing from American investors (who subsequently sold it on, no doubt at a handsome profit). Unfortunately for some, the wines of Lascombes, regardless of the improved quality, no longer taste like Margaux; others, however, have lapped them up. It is perhaps one of the greatest controversies in the appellation in recent years. Should a Margaux not taste like a Margaux?

Looking beyond to the troisièmes crus, tasting many vintages from the latter 20th century would reveal a similar litany of disappointments. Here, only Palmer has managed to produce wines that are regularly brilliant. Others, from this level and from lower rungs of the 1855 classification, are starting to catch up, though. Château d'Issan, for example, has started to turn out some very good wines. Nevertheless, for Margaux, inconsistency has been the watchword of the past few decades.

This inconsistency is particularly disheartening when one considers that Margaux has, of all the Médoc communes, perhaps the most readily identifiable style. St Estèphe is perhaps the most serious contender, with its hard, stony, gravelly

MY TOP TEN CHÂTEAUX

- Château Margaux
- Château Palmer
- Château Rauzan-Ségla
- Château Brane-Cantenac
- Château d'Issan
- Château Malescot St-Exupéry
- Château Lascombes
- Château Desmirail
- Château Giscours
- Château du Tertre

character. Pauillac and St Julien are less convincing contenders for the crown. Both have readily identifiable qualities, and accepting that each has, at various times and by various commentators, been described as the epitome of claret, I don't think they quite match a good Margaux for freshness of perfume. Nor would I want them to; this is about regional identity, typicité, if you will. This typicity, this perfume, must be related to the soils somehow; these are predominantly limestone, with clay, chalk and sand, but as is the case throughout the Médoc there are gravel croupes dotted here and there, and it is on these minor promontories that the best vineyards are to be found.

It is the perfume that marks a Margaux, a light yet gravelly quality, sometimes tempered by a palate of red fruits, sometimes darker, typically accompanied by an array of floral aromas, which at its best can be captivating, if not truly haunting. It is the apparent loss of these characteristics that are lamented, I think, in the new direction taken by certain properties at the turn of the century (or thereabouts) such as Kirwan and Lascombes. Personally, although I enjoy freshness and delineation in a wine and will always mark down wines that I feel are over-extracted, lacking focus and perhaps even lacking typicity, I do not find these wines to have gone too far for me to react in this way...yet. Although they offer much more impact and texture than they used to, I think the unique Margaux character is still there, underneath it all. But this is a personal thing; there are many who recoil in faux horror at the sight of the new bottles. I think it will be most interesting to see how these wines fare in ten years time; will the characteristics of the appellation and the terroir show through with age? With a few bottles in the cellar, I am looking forward to answering this question myself.

For details of all the Margaux châteaux, and how they were placed in the 1855 classification, see page 127.

St Julien

Although the commune is not blessed with a premier grand cru classé estate, as its neighbours to the north and south are, St Julien is in possession of a number of excellent properties at the deuxième cru level. Although each of these properties may have its detractors, and there are some points of criticism with which I would agree, some five estates are without doubt the standard bearers for the appellation, the figureheads behind which the rest of the commune marches. And they are responsible, in the case of Léoville-Las-Cases and Léoville-Barton for a long time, and for Léoville-Poyferré and Ducru-Beaucaillou only in more recent vintages, for some of the greatest wines in all Bordeaux.

A relatively small cluster of estates, St Julien is demarcated by the Chenal du Despartins and Jalle du Nord in the south (which separate the commune from an expanse of lesser land classified only as Haut-Médoc, the appellation of Margaux is further south again) and the Ruisseau de Juillac to the north, which marks the boundary with Pauillac. Here the two communes are contiguous, the vineyards of Château Léoville-Las-Cases lying next to those of the legendary Château Latour, a geographical fact that will surprise nobody who is a fan of St Julien's prime contender for first growth status, if only such a revision of the 1855 classification were ever possible. The terroir is much the same as it is in Margaux (please see page 113 for further description), although perhaps less varied. As a result of the drainage ditches carved out by 17th-century engineers, there is a huge sweep of gravel croupes, unbroken save for a small river which flows through the commune just to the south of Talbot, Langoa-Barton and Léoville-Barton.

As with Margaux, the châteaux of St Julien were subject to a classification in 1855, prior to the Exposition Universelle de Paris. My criticism is the same; this ranking is naturally of historical interest and acts as a useful framework for

MY TOP TEN CHÂTEAUX

- Château Ducru-Beaucaillou
- Château Léoville-Las-Cases
- Château Léoville-Poyferré
- Château Léoville-Barton
- Château Langoa-Barton
- Château Lagrange
- Château Saint-Pierre
- Château Gloria
- Château Beychevelle
- Château Branaire-Ducru

organising tastings and writing up notes, but it can no longer be described as a reliable guide to quality – 1855 is, after all, a long time ago, and much has changed since for the châteaux of Bordeaux. Nevertheless, perhaps in St Julien the guide is a shade more relevant – and helpful – than it is elsewhere in Bordeaux. There is greater consistency, and whether or not the châteaux all remain true to their 19th-century positions is probably more a matter of personal opinion here than it is in any other commune. Not everyone gets as much pleasure from wines such as Gruaud-Larose as they might from Ducru-Beaucaillou or one of the Léovilles, for instance, whereas others might even prefer Talbot. Nevertheless, I suspect most fans of this commune would not have to do too much shuffling (or drinking) before they came up with their own satisfactory listing.

Below classed growth level there are not too many estates of interest in the area, and this is perhaps not surprising as the aforementioned eleven classified properties account for 75% of the vines in the appellation, leaving little room for other producers of any true quality. One stand-out property is Château Gloria, not only for the wines but for its history. This estate was home to Henri Martin, and it began in 1942 with the purchase of just six hectares of vines. Over the ensuing years, assisted by his father Alfred, Henri went on to purchase more land, starting with a piece of the

Beychevelle vineyard continuing with parcels from Léoville-Poyferré, Gruaud-Larose, Léoville-Barton, Saint-Pierre, Lagrange, Ducru-Beaucaillou and even Duhart-Milon (a Pauillac property, but they owned a small plot in St Julien), until it reached a sizeable 48 hectares. The reputation of the wine was good, perhaps not surprising considering that the vineyard originated solely from land entitled to the grand cru classé label. Unfortunately for Martin, this title comes with the château, not with the vines, so despite his fine portfolio of vineyards he had no more right to use this title than he had when he

started. His only hope for Gloria was a reworking of the 1855 classification, an activity of which Martin was a strong exponent, but of course this has never happened. Martin did eventually realise his dream of classed growth ownership, however, with the acquisition of Château Saint-Pierre in 1982. Looking beyond Martin's creation, there are one or two other names to look out for, namely Lalande-Borie and Hortevie, but my recommendation would be that this is a commune where, other than Gloria, one should spend up for the wine of one of the more reasonably priced classed growth properties, if finances allow.

Pauillac

t is the combination of elegance and austerity that characterises St Julien, but in Pauillac we find something a little more fleshy, concentrated and, with some wines at least, a little more voluptuous. That is not to say the wines don't typify Bordeaux; they most certainly do, and the wines of both Pauillac and St Julien can age magnificently. But it is undeniable that those from Pauillac have their own character, utterly distinct from the great Léoville estates and their neighbours to the south, a character marked by aromas of fresh pencil shavings, cedar, blackcurrant, cigar-boxes and old wooden cabinets.

The appellation itself is effectively divided into two by the Chenal du Gaer, which flows past Artigues and then runs north of Grand-Puy-Ducasse to enter the Gironde just north of the town of Pauillac. To the south it is bounded by the Ruisseau de Juillac, which demarcates the transition from Pauillac to St Julien, whereas to the north the Jalle de Breuil provides a convenient boundary, on the other side of which lies St Estèphe. Between there are over 1,100 hectares of vines, and as this is the Médoc it is the gravel croupes that provide the best terroir, stony mounds on which the greatest estates are found. These waterways aid the drainage immeasurably,

although along the muddy banks of these rivers and streams themselves, as well as in the immediate vicinity of the Gironde, the land is completely unsuitable for the vine.

For many years Pauillac has provided the wine drinker with both ends of the quality spectrum; the magnificent wines of the first growths, especially Latour, but also serial under performance from some of the seemingly innumerable (in truth there are twelve) fifth growth estates. Wines like those from Pontet-Canet, Grand-Puy-Lacoste and Lynch-Bages can be superb, but others have much room for improvement, particularly the likes of Croizet-Bages and Lynch-Moussas. With the wave of

MY TOP TEN CHÂTEAUX

- Château Latour
- Château Lafite-Rothschild
- Château Mouton-Rothschild
- Château Pichon-Baron
- Château Pichon-Lalande
- Château Grand-Puy-Lacoste
- Château Pontet-Canet
- Château Lynch-Bages
- Château d'Armailhac
- Château Clerc-Milon

regeneration that has swept Bordeaux in the late 20th and early 21st century, however, and the renewed worldwide interest in wine, we can hope even these lesser properties raise their game and give us the wine we desire. If not, we can always look to the cru bourgeois properties of the appellation although Pauillac, as is the case with St Julien, is not awash with notable estates at this level.

Surprisingly, for what many would argue is the world's most significant wine region, Bordeaux is hardly a hotbed of culinary delights. In and around Pauillac, however, there are at least a few dishes of interest. The region is renowned for salt marsh lamb, the young animals having grazed on the aforementioned land alongside the Gironde, which is unsuitable for the vine. There are some notable restaurants in Pauillac, but nearby Bages is also of interest thanks to investment by Jean-Michel Cazes. Having grown up in the town, Cazes was looking to expand his wine storage facilities and was presented with the option of demolishing some of the vacant properties in the village and extending his already capacious warehouse. But he took a different path, and began to invest in the tiny village, restoring houses and shops. Today the village is a tourist attraction in itself. Jean-Michel has form for this, however, as the Cazes family own Bordeaux Saveurs, a company which specialises in Bordeaux hospitality, and he had already established a very successful hotel-restaurant at Château Cordeillan-Bages.

Naturally diners at these fine establishments are presented with a list of local wines to drink with their lamb, and looking beyond the first growths – and their eye-watering, wallet-melting prices – we could start with one of the two Pichon estates, Lalande and Baron, both of which are currently turning out superlative wines. There are

no estates ranked as troisième cru, but there are some decent wines made at fourth growth Duhart-Milon. As I have already mentioned, the bulk of Pauillac châteaux sit at the bottom of the 1855 classification, but here there are some truly excellent wines to be found which indicate just how foolish it can be to use this ancient listing as a guide to quality. I have found wines from d'Armailhac, Clerc-Milon, Grand-Puy-Lacoste, Lynch-Bages and Pontet-Canet to be excellent at one time or another, and many of the others can be superb value even if the absolute quality is not quite up with these first few. Both Haut-Bages-Libéral and Haut-Batailley certainly fit into this category. Of this brief listing, it is probably the resurgent Pontet-Canet that is worth getting to know; with a massive turn-around in the last decade of the 20th century, the wines now sit comfortably with those ranked as deuxième grand cru classé, and show an amazing concentration in some vintages.

Beyond the 1855 listing there are of course the cru bourgeois properties, although there are not many, and here Pibran probably ranks among the best. I have also tasted a few wines from La Fleur Peyrabon, which are sourced from a small five hectare plot within the Pauillac appellation, although they are vinified at Château Peyrabon, a Haut-Médoc estate. These wines, sadly, have not been so impressive.

St Estèphe

O ur arrival at St Estèphe marks the end of our journey through the four famous communes of the left bank of the Gironde. Travelling through Pauillac, we come to St Estèphe by crossing the Jalle de Breuil, one of the many drainage channels that have featured prominently in our journey north of Bordeaux. The terroir changes here, as although the best sites are located on the same gravel croupes as those found further to the south, underfoot there is a lot more clay, and thus the soils here are much more retentive of moisture than in Pauillac, St Julien or Margaux. Further to the north, beyond St Estèphe and the Chenal de Calon, are the supposedly lesser vineyards of the Médoc, sometimes referred to as the Bas-Médoc in order to distinguish them from those of the Haut-Médoc. The wines of St Estèphe have a distinctive character which may be directly correlated to these clay-rich soils. They tend towards greater richness in substance than those from further south, and the soils also confer a particular advantage in hot, dry years as the vines are less exposed to hydric stress than those vines grown in the more gravelly soils to the south, which are less retentive of water.

St Estèphe accounts for about 1,200 hectares, and thus is not significantly different in vineyard area to either Pauillac, which has about 1,100 hectares, or Margaux, which is a little larger with 1,300 hectares. Nevertheless, St Estèphe certainly has a very different profile. Unlike Pauillac and Margaux there is no premier grand cru classé estate to lead the way, and indeed the number of classed growth properties boasted by the commune is really very small. There are just five in all, half of the number found in St Julien which is considerably smaller at 900 hectares, and less than a third of that possessed by Pauillac. Nevertheless, although the quantity, at this level at least, may be low, the quality is not. Of these five estates, at least two, if not three or four, turn out truly superlative wines.

Leading the way in the St Estèphe appellation are Montrose and Cos d'Estournel, the latter frequently abbreviated by those familiar with the estate to Cos. Although both are renowned for the quality of their wines, this latter estate must surely also win the award for the most extravagant architecture in all Bordeaux. It is not that long since my eyes first caught sight of the château in real life, and it is just as striking in reality as it is in any picture. Sitting directly on the main road heading out of Pauillac, the château has a distinctly Oriental feel, with pagodas perched on top of the château built using golden sandstone, itself atypical for the region. The building was erected under the direction of Louis Gaspard d'Estournel, who was said to have been nicknamed the Maharajah of St Estèphe, a moniker that reflected his taste for travel to exotic climes, including India. Nevertheless the château, depicted on every label, certainly seems to have its roots in a country even further to the east.

Montrose, meanwhile, might at first consideration seem to have Scottish roots, but this is apparently not the case; the derivation of Montrose is uncertain, but it does not seem to be related to the beautiful Scottish coastal town of the same name. The best explanation of which I am aware is that mont-rose relates to the pink heather that once covered this small croupe of gravel. The vineyard here is relatively recent, and it was not until the early years of the 19th century,

MY TOP TEN CHÂTEAUX

- Château Montrose
- Château Cos d'Estournel
- Château Calon-Ségur
- Château Lafon Rochet
- Château Phélan-Ségur
- Château Haut-Marbuzet
- Château Tronquoy-Lalande
- Château Ormes de Pez
- Château Meyney
- Château de Pez

when the estate was inherited by Etienne Théodore Dumoulin, that vines were eventually planted. His attention was drawn to part of the estate, a plot of land to the south of the Calon vineyard and adjacent to the Gironde, entitled La Lande de l'Escargeon, the situation of which was such that it clearly had potential as a vineyard. Dumoulin did not hang about; having cleared the heather and scrub he established that the soil beneath was gravelly, and was eminently suited to the vine. By 1815 planting was underway, and by 1820 he had expanded the vineyard and had also built Montrose's rather bijou château. Only a few decades later, Montrose was ranked alongside Cos in the 1855 classification of the Médoc – a fantastic achievement.

Although these two grand estates occupy prime position in the commune, having both been ranked as deuxième cru in the 1855 classification, these are by no means the only names of interest. One step further down the 1855 ladder is Calon-Ségur, once part of the great and expansive Ségur estate of the 17th and 18th centuries, and although the wines have under-performed in many vintages of the 20th century, today it seems they are back on track, and can indeed be considered excellent. Just one rung down is Lafon-Rochet, which has been a very reliable source of good quality wine ever since the property was reinvigorated by the arrival of the Tesseron family, who have also done much to

bring Pontet-Canet in Pauillac back on track. At the lowest level, Cos Labory is one of those estates which could do better, but a number of vintages in the opening years of the 21st century have been well received and this is certainly an estate worth watching. And with the vineyards nestled between those of Cos d'Estournel, Lafon-Rochet and, just across the Jalle du Breuil, those of Lafite-Rothschild, it would seem that there is much unexploited potential here.

One characteristic that sets St Estèphe apart from near-neighbours St Julien and Pauillac is at the cru bourgeois level; St Estèphe is rich in such properties, many of which are sources of very good wine, often at a very good price. I expect everyone has their own favourite, and for years Meyney would have been top of many lists, helped by a very commendable wine in the 1989 vintage. Today the wines are still good, but not quite so enthralling perhaps, and there are new competitors; Phélan-Ségur is certainly worth investigating, as is Ormes de Pez, Haut-M should not be missed, and on occa Beau-Site can turn out a goo happy hunting grou classically st

Médoc

Beyond St Estèphe, across the Chenal de Calon, is the Médoc appellation. In terms of size this region of Bordeaux wipes the floor with those communal appellations to the south; whereas those typically have a thousand hectares each, give or take a few hundred, here we have 4,700 hectares eligible for the vine and the appellation. But size is not everything, of course; the reputation of the wines of the Médoc do not match those from the four leading communal appellations. This is largely down to the distinctly different terroir; here the gravel croupes have faded away, subsumed by rich, heavy, moisture-retentive soils. In many sections drainage channels dominate the landscape. And the vineyards are not as tightly packed as they are further south, intermingled as they are with woodland, and sometimes with other crops.

The clay-rich soils influence the decision on what varieties to plant, and the Merlot grape – which handles such soils better than Cabernet Sauvignon – is more predominant here than it is in St Estèphe, Pauillac, St Julien or Margaux. As a result of the Merlot-dominated blends, and of course the change in terroir, the wines have a different character to their more southerly neighbours. They may have a touch less finesse, but nevertheless there are plenty of good, although perhaps rather robust wines, a number of which have their ardent followers. Perhaps one of the most n⁓able is Potensac, which has been run for m⁓⁓s by the Delon family of Léovill⁓ ⁓he wines tend towards the stru⁓ but they can give ⁓ ⁓iently cellared. Other ⁓defunct ranking but ⁓e, I feel) estates 1855 this far ⁓xperienced ⁓ of ⁓t

MY TOP FIVE CHÂTEAUX

- Goulée
- Château Potensac
- Château Preuillac
- Château Rollan de By
- Château La Tour de By

Haut-Médoc including: Moulis & Listrac

This appellation is a very different animal altogether in comparison to the Médoc. Although roughly similar in size, at approximately 4,300 hectares, the land entitled to the appellation is strung out along the left bank and encapsulates the four famous communal appellations, as well as both Moulis and Listrac. The terroir is thus very variable but it does include a few small areas of gravel which are not included within the communal boundaries. There are five Haut-Médoc properties included in the 1855 classification, but also a great number of cru bourgeois estates, as well as a few that eschew any such classification whatsoever. Looking at those estates ranked in 1855 first, this small pack is undoubtedly led by La Lagune, a troisième cru sometimes wryly referred to as the premier grand cru of the region; not because of any desire to revise the 1855 classification, but because this is the first cru classé estate that one meets as one drives north out of Bordeaux on the D2. Almost next door is Cantemerle, which may not command the same level of interest amongst Bordeaux savants, but is frequently good value and only the ignorant overlook it.

The remaining three estates, Camensac, Belgrave and La Tour Carnet lie to the west of St Julien, and of this trio it is the latter that has the best reputation. But it is not only the classed growth estates that we should be looking out for. One vineyard that may well put all others to

Château Sociando-Mallet - vineyard and Gironde and nuclear power stations

shame is Sociando-Mallet, located just to the north of St Estèphe, before the boundary marking the switch from Haut-Médoc to Médoc. Home to Jean Gautreau and his family, this estate has been responsible for some of the most appealing wines of the appellation I have tasted.

Throughout the Haut-Médoc there are estates at the cru bourgeois level which are worthy of our attention. We all have our favourites, but of those that I have assessed in recent years I think Citran stands out as being of good quality, although both Beaumont and Caronne Ste-Gemme are chronically under-appreciated and are frequently smart buys, particularly in favourable vintages.

Not too far away from these Haut-Médoc estates are the communes of Moulis and Listrac, the two smallest and least appreciated of the left bank communes. Moulis, at just 550 hectares or thereabouts, is the smaller of the duo, although it boasts a number of high-flying cru bourgeois estates. Listrac, meanwhile, despite its 650 hectares is not associated with so many well known properties. In the former appellation, the best wines come from Poujeaux and Chasse-Spleen; in the latter of these two communes, Fourcas Hosten and Clarke are perhaps the two most notable names, and each occasionally provides us with some vinous pleasure.

MY TOP FIVE CHÂTEAUX
- Château La Lagune
- Château La Tour Carnet
- Château Sociando-Mallet
- Château Chasse-Spleen (Moulis)
- Château Poujeaux (Moulis)

St Emilion

Terroir matters everywhere, but here in St Emilion it seems much more apparent to the eye. Whereas the Médoc is a land of gently rolling hills, where an incline that climbs a mere 20 metres affords you a vantage point over much of the surrounding countryside, in the east of the St Emilion appellation, where the town lies, there is a more imposing escarpment, with many of the best vineyards located on the plateau – where the soils are rich in limestone – and on the slopes around the plateau, which are limestone and clay. This plateau is divided into two sections: to the west is the St Martin plateau, home to many of the leading estates of the appellation dotted around the town. To the east is the St Christophe plateau, extending eastwards towards the limit of the appellation; although the soils here are favourable the estates are not quite so prestigious.

The plateau and the slopes, or côtes as they are sometimes called, are two of the four important terroirs of the appellation. At the very western end of the appellation there is Graves-St-Emilion, the third and smallest of the four principal terroirs; here the vineyards are contiguous with those of Pomerol, and gravel soils predominate. The Gunzian graves de feu, the gravel after which this region of St Emilion is named, was borne to this place by the Isle and Dronne rivers and originates from the Quaternary period. It is gathered in five mounds, of which two bear the vines of Château Cheval Blanc, the remaining three being entirely Château Figeac. They have an altitude typically of 36 to 38 metres above sea level, and the gravelly soils are generally 7 to 8 metres deep; beneath this there is the clay that can be found throughout the region.

After limestone, clay and gravel comes sand, the fourth terroir that is typical of St Emilion. There are two main areas of sand; the first is stretched out across the plain to the west of the town of St Emilion and the limestone côtes. Here there are 1200 hectares of vineyards on aeolian (meaning eroded, transported and deposited by winds) sand, and it hosts a number of estates worthy of our attention, but none that yet – as far as the classification committee are concerned – challenge the upper echelons of the St Emilion ranking. Nevertheless, these are certainly not estates to be ignored; there are many properties here on the up, turning out wines of either excellent quality, excellent value, or indeed both. The second main area of sand is to the south of the town; here there are about 2,000 hectares available to the vine and again the terroir is sandy, but this time alluvial, having been

MY TOP TEN CHÂTEAUX

- Château Ausone
- Château Cheval Blanc
- Château Pavie
- Château Angélus
- Clos Fourtet
- Château Pavie-Macquin
- Château Larcis-Ducasse
- Château Figeac
- Château Grand-Mayne
- Château Beau-Séjour Bécot

deposited over the years by the Dordogne, which runs to the south.

Naturally even this subdivision into four terroirs is, in fact, a simplification; for example, the côtes are often thought of as a blending of limestone and clay, but in fact there are silty loam topsoils in places, sometimes sand, with a subsoil that may be more sandstone than limestone in places. Nevertheless, it is the terroirs where limestone, clay and gravel dominate that are of most interest. These regions play host to a collection of estates of superb repute, and indeed these soils might be regarded as sharing equal position at the very top of the St Emilion classification. There are two class A premier grand cru classé estates that preside over the St Emilion listing; Cheval Blanc on the gravel, and Ausone on the limestone and clay. The classification, unlike that of the properties of the Médoc which was set in stone (almost) in 1855, is open to review every ten years or so. Unfortunately this process does not run as smoothly as might be imagined, and the 2006 revision was subject to a legal challenge which seemingly put an end to the existence of any classification at all; only subsequent court rulings saved it. More details, including the reclassification debacle, are provided in my guide to the St Emilion classification on page 130.

The St Emilion regulations allow for a grand cru designation, although the term is misleading. In Burgundy this is the highest honour for any plot of land, a designation intrinsically intertwined with the terroir of the region. Here in St Emilion, where terroir is also vital, a wine qualifies for grand cru status based on little more than a few details of the harvest – a slightly lower yield and a minimum alcoholic strength of 11%... hardly pressing requirements. Thus the distinctions between St Emilion and St Emilion Grand Cru are very minor, rather akin to the difference between basic Bordeaux and Bordeaux Supérieur. As such, the grand cru designation is effectively meaningless to the consumer. More interesting are the grand cru classé and premier grand cru classé levels, designations awarded on behalf of the Minister for Agriculture and the Secretary of State. Both rankings are determined by committee, who make their judgements based on visits to the domaines in question and on tasting ten vintages. For the 2006 classification, the decision was made on the strength of the 1993-2002 vintages.

Pomerol

Although Pomerol has a long history of
viticulture and winemaking, it is not
one that has much in common with the
development of the left bank
appellations, or indeed with neighbouring St
Emilion. The vine has been cultivated on the right
bank, including at Pomerol, since the time of
Roman occupation. On the left bank viticulture in
Graves and Sauternes has flourished since
Medieval times, but in Pomerol it has waxed and
waned over time, while during the Hundred
Years' War the vineyards were abandoned
altogether. It was not until the 15th century that
there was any replanting, preceding the draining
of the Médoc by more than a hundred years.
Despite this, the region remained an obscure one
in viticultural circles, thought of by many as little
more than a satellite of the great St Emilion. There
was no influx of rich landlords as there was
around St Estèphe, Pauillac, St Julien and
Margaux; Pomerol had no Marquis Nicolas-
Alexandre de Ségur to name as the Prince des
Vignes, and no Baron Hector de Brane to christen

as Napoléon des Vignes. There were no wealthy
bankers or landed gentry interested in this rural
backwater, and thus the landscape remained one
dotted with farmhouses, criss-crossed by country
lanes, with no grand châteaux, no mansard roofs,
and barely a tiled turret to be seen.

The wines of this supposedly 'minor' region
were not widely appreciated, and the vignerons
and merchants that had settled here worked hard
to develop export markets for their wines. They
found buyers in France, Holland and particularly
Belgium, and the market they built up in the latter
country perhaps goes some way to explaining the
Belgian presence in Pomerol that exists today. The
wines of the left bank, however, were largely
exported to England, and thus British consumers
developed no awareness of Pomerol or the quality
of its wines. It was not until the 1950s that British
merchants woke up to the quality available, and
began importing to the UK, but even then the
prices of many of the wines were extremely
favourable, especially compared to the
astronomical prices some fetch today. And there is
one further difference
that marks out
Pomerol; whereas the
Médoc and Sauternes,
and subsequently
Graves and St Emilion,
were all classified
(arguably useless
classifications today,
but also without doubt
of great historical
importance), Pomerol
never underwent this
process, and today it
remains the only major
appellation of
Bordeaux to have no
classification.

Although small,
with just 784 hectares
– or thereabouts – of

vines, the terroir of Pomerol is certainly not homogenous, and is due some consideration. The vineyards are located to the west of St Emilion, and sit flush with the suburbs of Libourne. They are delimited north and south by two rivers, the Barbanne and the Taillas, to the east by the vineyards of St Emilion and the town of Pomerol itself, and to the west by the D910 as it runs down towards, and into, Libourne, with suburban streets forming the boundary. Further out in the appellation there is a subtle plateau which is dominated by gravel with clay, and it is these soil types that play host to the better vineyards. Inspection of the soils themselves reveals a considerable variation in gravel density and size of stone, even when comparing one vineyard to the next, although this isn't a feature unique to Pomerol by any means. A more significant change comes as you travel west through the appellation, when the soils become more sandy, and the quality of the wines may not be as high with this terroir. In addition, the clay subsoil here – known as crasse de fer – is particularly iron rich, and seams of it extend across the appellation. The Petrus vineyards are marked by it, as are those of Taillefer, the name of which translates literally as 'to cut iron'.

Like St Emilion, the clay soils here favour the Merlot grape which dominates the appellation, accounting for 80% of all the vines planted. Cabernet Sauvignon and Cabernet Franc trail in at the rear, although a few estates are notable for have significant plantings of these two varieties, sometimes accounting for more than half of the individual vineyard. Vieux Château Certan is a

good example, although even here Merlot still dominates, accounting for 60% of all the vines, with 30% Cabernet Franc and 10% Cabernet Sauvignon. The absolute predominance of Merlot in the appellation as a whole, however, may mean in some vintages the majority of the harvest can be lost. Merlot flowers slightly earlier than the two Cabernets and thus it is a lot more more vulnerable to spring frosts and reduced or irregular flowering and fruit set.

Although I have been content to criticise those that put too much stock in Bordeaux classifications, which are either outdated or rendered meaningless by internal political wrangling, one function that they do serve is to provide a loose framework for the discussion of the wines. Without one, I will not be inventing a classification of my own (you will be glad to hear), but I will provide a list of my My Top Ten châteaux, as I have done for all of the Bordeaux communes so far.

MY TOP TEN CHÂTEAUX

- Le Pin
- Petrus
- Château Lafleur
- Vieux Château Certan
- Château L'Église-Clinet
- Château Trotanoy
- Château L'Évangile
- Château Hosanna
- Château La Conseillante
- Château Clinet

Other regions

Any discussion of Bordeaux tends to focus on the grand châteaux, but it is worth remembering that these estates account for only a tiny proportion of the wine produced by the region. There are thousands of smaller estates, and there is value and interest waiting to be discovered everywhere. Sadly a pocket guide of this size cannot cover them in any great detail, but they deserve at least a brief mention.

The Côtes de Bordeaux, Côtes de Bourg and the Entre-deux-Mers

The new catch-all name for the Premières Côtes de Blaye, Premières Côtes de Bordeaux, Côtes de Francs and Côtes de Castillon appellations which came into being in 2007, the Côtes de Bordeaux is perhaps the first port of call for new and affordable Bordeaux. These disparate regions, of which two are right-bank regions (Francs, Blaye), the others (Castillon, Cadillac) sitting between the Garonne and Dordogne along with the Entre-deux-Mers, should still be identifiable from the communal names which will continue to be admissible on the label. Castillon is perhaps the best known of these, but hopefully not just because it is the location where the English were finally defeated by the French at the end of the Hundred Years' War; the slopes around the town have been recognised as a source of good value Bordeaux for many years.

The Côtes de Bourg was refused entry to the Bordeaux Côtes association following some quibbles over the use of the old appellation on the label, but here too there are some good wines to be found.

Fronsac & Canon-Fronsac

The quality attainable in these two appellations is no secret, and as long ago as the 18th century the wines of Fronsac were frequently served at the French court. With the arrival of phylloxera and the devastation of France's vineyards, however, Fronsac and the associated enclave Canon-Fronsac went into decline. Subsequently the region has seen hard times, hiding in the shadows of the limelight which today tends to focus on nearby Pomerol and St Emilion instead. Fortunately, investment from elsewhere in Bordeaux, and also from further afield, has benefited a number of properties.

St Emilion and Pomerol Satellites

Around St Emilion and Pomerol are a number of satellite appellations, Montagne-, Lussac-, Puisseguin- and St-Georges-St-Emilion, and of course close by there is also Lalande-de-Pomerol. With careful selection these regions may yield good value wines that offer an obvious Bordeaux fix at a decent price.

Generic Bordeaux

Tread with caution, but be aware that good value bottles can be found. The prime example has to be British expat Gavin Quinney, who at Château Bauduc makes an excellent Bordeaux Blanc and a decent red to match. Those prepared to do a little digging will reap the rewards.

MY TOP TEN CHÂTEAUX

- Château Lezongars (Premières)
- Domaine de l'A (Castillon)
- Château d'Aiguilhe (Castillon)
- Château Veyry (Castillon)
- Château Roc de Cambes (Bourg)
- Château Bauduc (AC Bordeaux)
- Château Canon de Brem (Fronsac)
- Château de la Rivière (Fronsac)
- Château la Vieille Cure (Fronsac)
- Château Thieuley (AC Bordeaux)

1855 Médoc

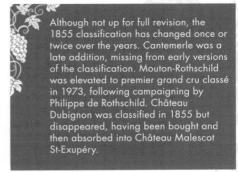

Although not up for full revision, the 1855 classification has changed once or twice over the years. Cantemerle was a late addition, missing from early versions of the classification. Mouton-Rothschild was elevated to premier grand cru classé in 1973, following campaigning by Philippe de Rothschild. Château Dubignon was classified in 1855 but disappeared, having been bought and then absorbed into Château Malescot St-Exupéry.

Napoleon III, having decided that the great wines of Bordeaux should be featured in the Exposition Universelle de Paris of 1855, asked the brokers of the region to draw up a list of properties ranked into five groups according to quality. But quality is perhaps rather nebulous, and the pragmatic businessmen decided to rank the wines according to price, which no doubt seemed to those charged with the task to be an appropriate surrogate. Although intended as a listing for the show, and nothing more, the classification stuck fast and appears to be with us for the rest of eternity.

Premiers Crus
- Château Lafite-Rothschild
- Château Latour
- Château Mouton-Rothschild
- Château Margaux
- Château Haut-Brion

Deuxièmes Crus
- Château Pichon-Baron
- Château Pichon-Lalande
- Château Ducru-Beaucaillou
- Château Gruaud-Larose
- Château Léoville-Las Cases
- Château Léoville-Barton
- Château Léoville-Poyferré
- Château Cos d'Estournel
- Château Montrose
- Château Brane-Cantenac
- Château Durfort-Vivens
- Château Lascombes
- Château Rauzan-Ségla
- Château Rauzan-Gassies

Troisièmes Crus
- Château Lagrange
- Château Langoa-Barton
- Château Boyd-Cantenac
- Château Cantenac-Brown
- Château Desmirail
- Château Ferrière
- Château Giscours
- Château d'Issan
- Château Kirwan
- Château Malescot St-Exupéry
- Château Marquis d'Alesme
- Château Palmer
- Château Calon-Ségur
- Château La Lagune

Quatrièmes Crus
- Château Duhart-Milon
- Château Marquis-de-Terme
- Château Pouget
- Château Prieuré-Lichine
- Château Beychevelle
- Château Branaire-Ducru
- Château St Pierre
- Château Talbot
- Château Lafon Rochet
- Château La Tour Carnet

Cinquièmes Crus
- Château d'Armailhac
- Château Batailley
- Château Clerc-Milon
- Château Croizet-Bages
- Château Grand-Puy-Ducasse
- Château Grand-Puy-Lacoste
- Château Haut-Bages-Libéral
- Château Haut-Batailley
- Château Lynch-Bages
- Château Lynch-Moussas
- Château Pédesclaux
- Château Pontet-Canet
- Château Dauzac
- Château du Tertre
- Château Cos-Labory
- Château Belgrave
- Château Camensac
- Château Cantemerle

1855 Sauternes

t seems that the years running up to the Exposition Universelle de Paris in 1855 were indeed busy for the merchants of Bordeaux. That they were charged with drawing up a new classification of the red wines of the Médoc, in order to facilitate showing the wines at the exhibition, is well known. It is easy to forget, however, that the sweet wines of Sauternes and Barsac were classified along with their red counterparts. As with the wines of the Médoc, these wines were classified according to market value at the time.

Premier Cru Supérieur
- Château d'Yquem

Premiers Crus
- Château Climens
- Château Coutet
- Château Guiraud
- Clos Haut-Peyraguey
- Château Lafaurie-Peyraguey
- Château Rabaud-Promis
- Château de Rayne-Vigneau
- Château Rieussec
- Château Sigalas-Rabaud
- Château Suduiraut
- Château La Tour-Blanche

Deuxièmes Crus
- Château d'Arche
- Château Broustet
- Château Caillou
- Château Doisy-Daëne
- Château Doisy-Dubroca
- Château Doisy-Védrines
- Château Filhot
- Château Lamothe
- Château Lamothe-Guignard
- Château de Malle
- Château de Myrat
- Château Nairac
- Château Romer du Hayot
- Château Suau

With all such classifications the first question is relevance. What does this classification mean to us today? I would argue very little. The wines were classified to inform those visiting an exhibition (held more than 150 years ago) as to which wines should impress most, assuming those that cost the most offered greatest quality. Today, the world is populated by a very different body of consumers. Those that maintain an interest in Sauternes buy on tasting experience, track record and published critical reviews. It may be that many of the high ranking properties continue to dominate the trade, that the premier cru estates on the whole tend to be better known, and still make the better wines. But these days this is an easily challengeable assertion. There are a number of wines from the 1855 classification that frequently disappoint, and there are also many wines not classified that punch well above their weight.

1959 Graves

T he 1855 classifications of the Médoc, Sauternes and Barsac ignored what are undoubtedly very important regions of Bordeaux, notably St Emilion, Pomerol and Graves. This latter exclusion is perhaps somewhat surprising, as the wines of Graves were well known at the time, as evinced by the inclusion of Haut-Brion at the first growth level in the Médoc classification. Determined to protect and promote the identity of the region, the Graves Syndicat were eager to put forward their own classification, although they were not able to achieve this until almost a century had passed.

Most resources refer to an initial classification having been drawn up in 1953 and subsequently ratified in 1959, but it appears this might be an erroneous view. The 1953 classification was official, following its ratification by ministerial decree in 1958 (source: the Syndicat des Crus Classés de Graves). The classification was then renewed the following year, with the addition of five new wines (the whites Couhins, Latour-Martillac and Malartic-Lagravière, and the reds Fieuzal and Pape-Clément). It is this 1959 classification that has been carried through to modern day, with no significant changes.

Château La Tour-Haut-Brion is no more; part of the Haut-Brion portfolio which has seen some rationalisation in recent years, the final vintage was in 2004. From 2005 the fruit is used in the second wine of Château La Mission Haut-Brion.

Graves, 1959: Classified - White

- Château Bouscaut
- Château Carbonnieux
- Domaine de Chevalier
- Château Couhins
- Château Couhins-Lurton
- Château Latour-Martillac
- Château Malartic-Lagravière
- Château Laville-Haut-Brion
- Château Olivier

Graves, 1959: Classified - Red

- Château Bouscaut
- Château Carbonnieux
- Domaine de Chevalier
- Château de Fieuzal
- Château Haut-Bailly
- Château Haut-Brion
- Château Latour-Martillac
- Château Malartic-Lagravière
- Château La Mission Haut-Brion
- Château Olivier
- Château Pape-Clément
- Château Smith-Haut-Lafitte
- Château La Tour-Haut-Brion

The issue of Haut-Brion sometimes causes some confusion as to its ranking in Bordeaux classifications. The château was ranked along with those of the Médoc in 1855 as a first growth, although obviously this applies only to its red wine – there is no such thing as a white Médoc, after all. The estate was also included in the Graves classification in 1953, although again only for its red wine – the white wine is produced in such tiny quantities that, like the proprietors of Fieuzal, the Dillon family at Haut-Brion did not ask for its inclusion. Several sources have since reported that the white wine was then retrospectively incorporated into the classification in 1960, although today the Dillon family deny that this is the case.

2006 St Emilion

This classification was first published on the 16th June 1955 and subsequently amended by decree the following August and October, the final list having 12 properties ranked as Premier Grand Cru Classé and 63 as Grand Cru Classé. The system was then revised in 1969, and again in 1986 and 1996. The most recent revision in 2006, which saw eleven châteaux demoted, saw the classification dogged by legal challenge and controversy.

The only workable solution was to find a ranking that would keep everybody content. This took more than three years to enact, and eventually in May 2009 a new law concerning the classification was passed which kept the 2006 promotions and conveniently overlooked the demotions. Result? The promoted are promoted and are thus happy, the demoted haven't been demoted and are thus happy.

Until the next time, of course. The current state of play – the 1996 classification with 2006 promotions – is due for review in 2012.

Premiers Grands Crus Classés - A
- Château Ausone
- Château Cheval-Blanc

Premiers Grands Crus Classés - B
- Château Angélus
- Château Beau-Séjour Bécot
- Château Beauséjour (Duffau-Lagarrosse)
- Château Bélair-Monange
- Château Canon
- Château Figeac
- Clos Fourtet
- Château La Gaffelière
- Château Magdelaine
- Château Pavie
- Château Pavie-Macquin*
- Château Troplong-Mondot*
- Château Trottevieille

Grands Crus Classés
- Château L'Arrosée
- Château Balestard-La-Tonnelle
- Château Bellefont-Belcier*
- Château Bellevue†

- Château Bergat
- Château Berliquet
- Château Cadet-Bon†
- Château Cadet-Piola
- Château Canon-la-Gaffelière
- Château Cap-de-Mourlin
- Château Chauvin
- Château La Clotte
- Château Corbin
- Château Corbin-Michotte
- Château La Couspaude
- Couvent des Jacobins
- Château Dassault
- Château Destieux*
- Château La Dominique
- Château Faurie-de-Souchard†
- Château Fleur-Cardinale*
- Château Fonplégade
- Château Fonroque
- Château Franc-Mayne
- Château Grand-Corbin*
- Château Grand-Corbin-Despagne*
- Château Grand-Mayne
- Château Grand-Pontet
- Château Les Grandes-Murailles
- Château Guadet St-Julien†

- Château Haut-Corbin
- Château Haut Sarpe
- Clos des Jacobins
- Château Laniote
- Château Larcis-Ducasse
- Château Larmande
- Château Laroque
- Château Laroze
- Château La Marzelle†
- Château Matras
- Château Monbousquet*
- Château Moulin-du-Cadet
- Clos de l'Oratoire
- Château Pavie-Decesse
- Château Petit-Faurie-de-Soutard†
- Château Le Prieuré
- Château Ripeau
- Château St-Georges-Côte-Pavie
- Clos St-Martin
- Château La Serre
- Château Soutard
- Château Tertre-Daugay†
- Château La Tour-du-Pin†
- Château La Tour-du-Pin-Figeac† (Moueix)
- Château La Tour Figeac
- Château Villemaurine†
- Château Yon-Figeac†

*châteaux promoted in 2006 who maintained their new positions
†châteaux originally demoted in 2006, but who maintained their previous positions following a prolonged legal process

Cru Bourgeois

The recent history of the Cru Bourgeois designation has been a troubled one. A well-meaning revision of the classification in the early years of the 21st century led to one legal challenge after another and, as with any system that has taken such a battering, collapse was the eventual outcome.

Although a painful process, from the classification's ashes rose a new system, an annually renewed selection of wines deemed worthy of the Cru Bourgeois designation, the process overseen by the Alliance des Crus Bourgeois du Médoc. The process begins for each vintage with two committees, one for the Médoc and one for the communal appellations. These committees determine the quality level for the vintage in question, and set the criteria by which the wines are to be judged. Each property submitting a wine will be visited to establish eligibility which, once agreed, can be suspended or withdrawn as deemed necessary following unannounced spot-checks of the estate.

Further meetings of the Alliance in 2008 seemed to ratify the process as above, with nearly 300 estates opting in to this new, annually awarded accolade in its first year (the 2008 vintage). Any estate with at least 7 hectares in the Haut-Médoc or 4 hectares in one of the communal appellations such as Pauillac would be eligible to apply. There were some concerns, especially as the new award stipulated barrel and vat capacities, meaning some estates needed to make significant investments before qualifying. Nevertheless, on the whole, it appears the producers moved forward together in a positive fashion. There have been two vintages assessed for this system; but with several hundred châteaux qualifying, there are too many to list here.

The 2011 Unofficial Liv-Ex Classification

S ince the 1855 classification was drawn up there have been countless unofficial attempts to redraft it, none of which can really be considered successful. Until 2009 that is, when the Liv-Ex revision was published. This particular reworking of the 1855 classification seems to have struck a chord, and the significance of this was emphasised when the list was revised in 2011, thus facilitating a comparison not only of interest to wine historians, but also showing us, the general public, how wines have changed in value over the last couple of years. Like the original 1855 classification it is based on price, but unlike the original it allows for all the châteaux of Pessac-Léognan, not just Haut-Brion.

THE 2011 LISTING IS AS FOLLOWS:

Premiers Crus
- Château Lafite-Rothschild
- Château Latour
- Château Margaux
- Château Mouton-Rothschild
- Château Haut-Brion
- Château La Mission Haut Brion

Deuxièmes Crus
- Château Palmer
- Château Léoville-Las-Cases
- Château Cos d'Estournel
- Château Ducru-Beaucaillou
- Château Duhart-Milon
- Château Lynch-Bages
- Château Pichon-Lalande
- Château Montrose
- Château Pape-Clément
- Château Pontet-Canet
- Château Pichon-Baron
- Château Beychevelle

Troisièmes Crus
- Château Léoville-Poyferré
- Château Haut-Bailly
- Château Léoville-Barton
- Château Lascombes
- Château Rauza-Ségla
- Château Malescot St-Exupéry
- Château Calon-Ségur
- Château Smith-Haut-Lafitte
- Château Clerc-Milon
- Château Grand-Puy-Lacoste

Quatrièmes Crus
- Château Cantenac-Brown
- Château Branaire-Ducru
- Château d'Issan
- Château Brane-Cantenac
- Domaine de Chevalier
- Château Saint-Pierre
- Château Gruaud-Larose
- Château La Lagune
- Château Giscours
- Château Kirwan

- Château Talbot
- Château Langoa-Barton
- Château d'Armailhac
- Château Lagrange
- Château Boyd Cantenac

Cinquièmes Crus
- Château Batailley
- Château Pouget
- Château Malartic-Lagravière
- Château Rauzan-Gassies
- Château Dauzac
- Château Prieuré-Lichine
- Château Haut-Marbuzet
- Château Haut Bages Libéral
- Château Ferrière
- Château Grand Puy Ducasse
- Château Sociando-Mallet
- Château Durfort-Vivens
- Château Marquis de Terme
- Château Lafon-Rochet
- Château Haut-Batailley
- Château du Tertre

11

Enjoying Bordeaux

You've paid good money for that bottle of Bordeaux you're about to open; you need to make sure you get the very best out of it. This chapter gives some guidance in this respect. After a quick recap on Bordeaux labels, I offer some words of advice on everything from cellaring Bordeaux, keeping track of your bottles, advice on the best wine glasses, decanting, tasting and I even offer some thoughts on what foods are best with Bordeaux.

Reading a Bordeaux Wine Label

Bordeaux has not evolved into the multi-parcellated patchwork of vines and vineyards that we see in some other wine regions, most notably Burgundy or much of Germany. Here the château is king, each estate effectively a brand name for the wine produced from its network of vineyards which may expand or contract over time, as plots of vines are bought, sold or exchanged. The unfortunate effect of this is that we don't have the granularity that we get in Burgundy or Germany; we consumers don't get a chance to focus in on individual plots of vines, individually named vineyards, and get to grips with the wines these vines produce. That is our loss. There is, however, one benefit of this lower level of complexity, and that is significantly simpler labelling.

There is little on any typical Bordeaux wine label that should confuse. Nevertheless, here are a handful of pointers.

Château Haut Brion is one of the five first growths of Bordeaux. Here the label shows an image of the château, and below the name of the château is the vintage, 1990. This is printed in a different colour as the same label design is used year after year, the vintage printed on afterwards as required. The term Cru Classé de Graves denotes this château's position in the Graves classification system. This château was the only Graves château to be included in the 1855 classification of left bank châteaux, as denoted by Premier Grand Cru Classé en 1855. The appellation, Pessac-Léognan, an enclave of Graves, is also declared.

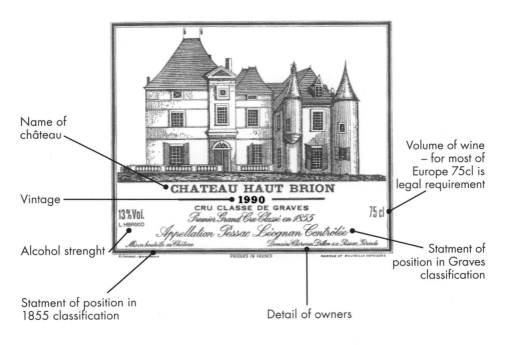

Name of château

Vintage

Alcohol strenght

Statment of position in 1855 classification

Volume of wine – for most of Europe 75cl is legal requirement

Statment of position in Graves classification

Detail of owners

Cellaring Bordeaux

H aving developed a taste for Bordeaux it will not be very long before you have to consider where to store your many bottles as they mature; drinking the odd bottle in its adolescent youth is fine, but if you really want to see a complexity worthy of the price tag, Bordeaux commands that you squirrel some of your bottles away for a few years. This may seem eminently impracticable, but I assure you that a wine 'cellar' is not the sole reserve of the rich or titled. Anyone, whether living in a flat or a similarly cellar-less modern semi-detached house can, with a little ingenuity, 'cellar' wine. What matters is having some knowledge of the features of a good cellar, and putting this knowledge into practice. And if there remain insurmountable obstacles to the long-term storage of wine at home, fear not, for there are other storage options available to you.

The greatest issue affecting wine when stored over many years is temperature. The ideal temperature is 10C to 13C, but several degrees either side of this is quite safe. In fact, provided

the wines do not freeze, which does not occur until the temperature drops some way below 0C (the alcohol acts as an antifreeze), then it is quite safe for temperatures to drop lower than the ideal. A little above 13C is also quite safe, and I would be happy with wines stored medium term in temperatures up to about 15C; this will not spoil the wines at all. With even higher temperatures, up to 18C, many wines will still survive in the short term, although I do not recommend such temperatures for even medium-term storage.

Temperature fluctuation is another great concern; the oscillation between hot and cold that might result from the proximity of a boiler or hot water pipes will soon cause irrevocable damage. Fluctuations taking place over the day (alternating between a warm day and a cool night) may be just as unhealthy. Fluctuations over the course of the year (cooler in winter, warmer in the summer) are, in my experience, of no consequence, provided the absolute temperature does not rise too high, as the change is too gradual to have any great effect on the wine.

The ideal wine cellar should also have low levels of light and vibration. Humidity is also said to be important, but I am not so convinced. So take a look around; is there anywhere in the home – the back of a garage perhaps – that, suitably insulated and made secure, could serve as your 'cellar'. If so, all well and good, but if not then you need to consider one of the other options available to you.

OTHER STORAGE OPTIONS:

- **WINE CABINETS:** dedicated units holding several hundred bottles.
  For: perfect storage conditions.
  Against: bulky, expensive, electricity charges.
- **SPIRAL CELLAR:** a prefabricated cellar sunk below ground.
  For: excellent conditions, large capacity.
  Against: expensive, and non-portable.
- **OFFSITE STORAGE:** pay a merchant or dedicated company to store your wine.
  For: ensures perfect provenance.
  Against: usually cases only, annual storage fees, wines are not accessible.

Bordeaux – Keeping Track of Your Wine

So you are accruing bottles with abandon, and burying them away in whatever makeshift cellar you have created. The problem is, how can you keep track of your stock? Without some plan, you will soon find yourself in the possession of a huge pile of bottles, no idea what lies at the bottom, no idea how much you have drunk and no idea what remains from any particular purchase. I can also guarantee you will never be able to find that one particular bottle you are looking for, until you uncover it by chance a week later, the moment when you wanted to drink it having long since passed.

Flip through the pages of any general wine guide from ten or more years ago for a solution to this problem and the author is almost certain to direct you to a cellar book, perhaps even a rather ornate leather-bound one. Today, however, there are many more attractive options than notebook and pen; with the arrival of the home computer wine storage records went electronic, and with the arrival of the internet they have gone global. Online applications not only allow you to store details of your wine purchases and bottles consumed, but also to see what professional critics are saying about the wines in your cellar. And, as if that weren't enough, you can see what other drinkers who have bought the same wines as you are saying about it, taking your knowledge of the wines to a level way beyond what any paper-based system could achieve.

Without a doubt the best option is CellarTracker! (www.cellartracker.com), an online application run by ex-Microsoft engineer and wine lover Eric LeVine. The site is free to use although I would encourage the payment of the optional annual donation; Eric's excellent and ground-breaking service certainly warrants it. Your list of wines can be entered by hand, imported from spreadsheet or even recorded using barcode technology. Once in, the features are endless; you can access the details of your cellar from anywhere in the world, by computer or mobile phone. You can decide what and when to drink based on a multitude of published opinions from professional critics (including my own notes, over 10,000 of which are held in CellarTracker!) and fellow drinkers (by the end of 2011 CellarTracker! users had recorded more than 2.3 million tasting notes online). And if you choose to add your tasting notes to the CellarTracker! database, you contribute to this huge repository of knowledge and opinion; you can also send your notes out to Facebook and Twitter. It is a fabulous site which has revolutionised not just record keeping, but wine communication.

Serving Bordeaux – Temperature and Decanting

I n times gone by, before wines were routinely fined and filtered to a crystal clear state, it was quite common for wines poured from both barrel and bottle to contain a considerable degree of solid matter. In order to avoid bringing an unsightly looking wine to the table, it was quite the norm to decant the wine into a suitably resplendent container. The need for such a receptacle led to the development of the many and varied elegant decanters which are available today on the market. But who actually owns a decanter nowadays? People who live in stately homes, or perhaps the proprietors of antique and curiosity shops? No, not at all. Anyone who wants the best from their wine, especially when that wine is a carefully matured bottle from Bordeaux, should own one. Decanting wine is not just for show, there are at least two very specific benefits.

Wines which have aged in the bottle, typically red wines rather than white, will start producing a sediment after a period of time. This is the first reason wine should be decanted, to separate the wine from these undesirable solids. The second reason is to allow the wine some contact with the air – sometimes this is referred to as letting the wine breathe – in order for the aromas and flavours to develop. If you are in any doubt as to the need for mature and maturing Bordeaux to breathe, fill a decanter or similar vessel with your next bottle and taste every half hour or so. The evolution of aromas, flavours and texture will surprise you. As a general rule, the younger the wine, the longer it takes; I find classed growth Bordeaux that is just beginning to drink well, say at 10-12 years of age, often needs three to four hours before it shows well. Once past 15 years of age often just a couple of hours will do it. Ancient wines might be best not decanted at all,

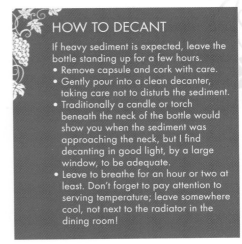

HOW TO DECANT

If heavy sediment is expected, leave the bottle standing up for a few hours.
- Remove capsule and cork with care.
- Gently pour into a clean decanter, taking care not to disturb the sediment.
- Traditionally a candle or torch beneath the neck of the bottle would show you when the sediment was approaching the neck, but I find decanting in good light, by a large window, to be adequate.
- Leave to breathe for an hour or two at least. Don't forget to pay attention to serving temperature; leave somewhere cool, not next to the radiator in the dining room!

whereas younger wines may well need even more than four hours.

One important point to realise is that you don't need one of those expensive, lead crystal, antique decanters to do the job; decanters really don't need to be complicated or expensive to serve well. Clearly there are pricy, hand-blown crystal options on the market, and there's nothing wrong with using one of those should your budget allow. But remember that our two principal aims are removal of sediment and contact with the air; both can be achieved by decanting into a simple glass jug, if necessary. Once ready for drinking the wine will naturally be poured into wine glasses, and this is where your should spend up; good quality wine glasses do a lot to improve your wine experience. So don't worry about what you decant into; what matters is that you decant at all, not how fancy your decanter is.

Wine Glasses for Bordeaux

n order to get the most enjoyment out of your Bordeaux, and indeed any wine, it is necessary to give at least a little thought to choosing the wine glasses that you plan to use. There are a number of manufacturers of fine, and somewhat expensive, crystal glasses, designed specifically for use with certain wines. It's not necessary to break the bank, however, but it is worth splashing some cash for glasses that at least meet the basic criteria described below.

A BRIEF GUIDE TO THE GLASS

Material

At the very least, the wine glass must be plain and clear. Enjoyment of wine includes the appreciation of colour, as it can impart a lot of information about the wine. Consequently, wine glasses made from coloured or frosted glass are useless. I personally feel that overly ornate cut crystal is also detrimental to the appearance of the wine, especially as such glasses are often far too small and the wrong shape. I find plain lead crystal glass to be best, as this material is not only clear but also sufficiently strong for the glass to have a pleasingly thin rim.

Shape and Size

The glasses should be of a sufficient size; the bowl should be large enough to allow a fair measure to be poured, whilst leaving enough room for the wine to be gently swirled without the risk of spilling. This swirling action is to release aromas from the wine, and is therefore vitally important. Wine glasses that are so tiny that they must be filled to the brim in order to achieve a decent measure are plainly inadequate. Traditionally, the shape should taper in towards the top so that the aperture is narrower than the bowl lower down, a shape which is said to concentrate the aromas at the top of the glass. I'm not so sure about that, but it is much easier to swirl in this style of glass than a wide-brimmed design.

Stems

In my opinion the glass should have a stem, mainly because then it can be held without covering the bowl in greasy fingerprints. Having said that, I know I am a little old-fashioned in this respect, and some leading glass manufacturers such as Riedel are producing wine glasses without stems. Personally I prefer the traditional design, but the shape and material of these stemless glasses are otherwise fine, so if you prefer that model, by all means follow your nose.

Cleaning

Looking after your glasses is easy; glasses should be washed between use, and although some advocate using hot water alone, I would advise using detergent, otherwise glasses simply gather dirt. Just ensure the glasses are thoroughly rinsed afterwards, as even a trace washing-up liquid can ruin a wine. Alternatively, many glasses are dishwasher safe, and this seems the perfect cleaning method to me, especially when you have dozens of dirty glasses to wash up!

Tasting Bordeaux

Perhaps this section should be entitled 'Wine Appreciation', because there is a lot more to enjoying the wines of Bordeaux than merely 'tasting'. Let's have a look at how it's done.

Look

It is worth taking a good look at the wine, as its appearance can yield a lot of information. It's best to view the wine against a white background, in order to avoid mistaking the colour. This doesn't have to be anything technical – a white plate or tablecloth will do. The colour of a red wine will give a clue as to the age of the wine. Many red wines start life as a deep purple colour, sometimes almost opaque, taking on a paler, tawny, brick red hue with age. Similar information may be gathered from inspecting a white wine, although the pattern of colour change as a white wine ages is different. A good example is Sauternes; this wine starts off a lemon-gold colour, but will deepen with age, turning a rich amber hue and eventually a golden-brown. In both cases these changes are gradual, occurring over many, many decades.

Smell

Swirl the glass to throw the wine up the side of the glass, thus increasing the surface area of wine in contact with the air. It is at the interface between wine and air that aromas are released, and thus increasing the surface area helps to make the aromas more apparent. The agitation of the wine also helps. Once done, stick your nose in the glass, take a good sniff, and try to analyse what aromas rise up from the wine as you do so. Young wines will have primary aromas, relating to the grape variety. Such smells are often fruit related, blackcurrants and damsons for young red Bordeaux perhaps, and maybe pineapple and vanilla for Sauternes. As wines age more

secondary aromas develop, which may be more complex. The aromas generated by a glass of mature Bordeaux, red or white, are many, and this is the reason why these wines come at a premium.

Taste

There is a lot more to describe when tasting the wine than simple flavour. On the 'palate' (the term used to describe the characteristics of the wine detected in the mouth) other elements come into play. Detecting the absolute presence and relative quantities of these substances tells you about quality, ageing potential, how well the wine will drink with food, and so on. Watch out for the mouth-coating furring of tannins in a young red Bordeaux, the sharpness of the acidity on the tip of the tongue, and how all these elements fit together – in other words, how well balanced the wine is. Don't be afraid to slurp a little, and release the aromas in the mouth, and pay attention to the sensations derived from swallowing the wine – known as the finish. The longer it lasts the better the wine!

Bordeaux and Food

There are two basic rules worth remembering when matching wine with food, and they illustrate quite nicely two simple themes of this art. Combining a fresh and acidic white wine with a rich, oily fish dish is an example of contrast, where the wine is different in character to the food, yet still complementary. The combination of a sweet wine with a rich dish is an example of food and wine complementing one another, both working together through their similar traits.

If this already sounds a little complex, fear not. Wine and food work well together in general – with only a few combinations that really don't click. What is more important is to memorise the wine and food combinations that don't work (and should be avoided), rather than those that do.

No red Bordeaux with fish…usually

Red Bordeaux is generally a tannic style of wine, and these tannins, in combination with a fish dish, will impart an unpleasant, pseudo-metallic taste to the wine. The same can be said for many red wine and cheese combinations, a match that many find agreeable, but I rarely enjoy. Consequently, most fish dishes will be best served with white Bordeaux, especially dry white Bordeaux, but also sweet wines such as Sauternes. These wines do not have the tannins that are so detrimental to the experience, and the acidity helps to cut through the sometimes oily richness of the dish.

One exception to this rule is Lamproie a la Bordelaise, a traditional Bordeaux dish featuring lampreys – eel-like creatures – stewed and

preserved in red wine. There's no doubt that this rich and meaty dish works best with a red wine.

No dry Bordeaux with sweet foods

I think paying attention to sweetness in food and wine is paramount, allowing for both complementary and contrasting matches. The latter, though, should never involve a dry wine with sweet food. Sugar-rich foods swamp the palate, changing the way a dry wine tastes. The opposite can work very well though; Sauternes with blue cheese, Stilton, Roquefort or otherwise, is a classic example of a contrasting combination, and the other classic duo – Sauternes with foie gras – is a highly complementary match. Watch out for drinking Sauternes with dessert though – you might think it would work well, but I find it does the wine no favours.

Sauternes is in fact much more versatile than these few words suggest. I have enjoyed it with roast chicken, and it works very well with oysters, sushi and all manner of Asian cuisines. Once you see past the idea of Sauternes as a 'dessert wine', the possibilities are endless.

12

Money
Matters

In this final chapter I get to grips with the financial side of buying and drinking Bordeaux. I offer some advice on where to buy, including my thoughts on the modern en primeur system, as well as taking a closer look at professional storage as an alternative to cellaring wine in your own home. I finish up with a summary of what has happened to the value of Bordeaux on the market during 2011, complimenting my review of that vintage on page 29.

Buying Bordeaux

I n many parts of the world the wine trade is an established business, and your nearest independent wine merchant will have plenty of different options for you to peruse. But there are other routes to buying Bordeaux which may be financially beneficial. Here is a guide to some of the various buying opportunities for you to consider.

The Independent Wine Merchant

First, let's not overlook our local bricks-and-mortar retailers; if you have a local merchant, then I urge you to get to know them; the proprietor, the staff, their list and when their offers come out. Tap into their knowledge and your wine life will be all the richer for it. If they offer tastings, get in on them; the best way to learn about wine, and your own taste preferences, is to taste, taste, taste. There's no substitute for it.

The Internet

Once you would have had to chase up distant merchants to send you their list, making your orders by telephone or written word: naturally, these days are long gone. The internet has revolutionised wine retail; no self-respecting merchant of Bordeaux, or indeed any other wine, would be without a presence on the web. In the vast majority of cases an e-commerce service will be included, so that you can buy at the click of a button. Get on their email list to hear of their sales and other offers; you might just pick up that vintage of Château Haut-Bailly you were after at a significantly reduced rate.

At Auction

Wine auctions aren't just for crusty old toffs shopping at Christie's or Sotheby's; there are many smaller provincial auction houses in existence selling wine alongside their art, property and even livestock! Take a look in your local classifieds to see if there are any near you; or indeed, if there are any more distant accepting bids by telephone or email. Bargains can be secured this way – I know from personal experience! Even here, the internet has pushed things forward; there are now dedicated online wine auction companies (www.winebid.com, www.bidforwine.com) that are worth a look.

Visiting Bordeaux

For many of France's wine regions a great way to buy is to visit – you can taste the wine, meet the people that made it, walk in the vineyard, and usually purchase at a reduced price. Because of the complex system by which Bordeaux comes to market, however (see page 104), this simply doesn't work in Bordeaux. The top châteaux are increasingly open to receiving visitors these days – by appointment only – for a tour and perhaps a small tasting, but don't expect to buy the wine at the château. That which was intended for sale has long gone to the region's courtiers and négociants.

An important aspect of buying Bordeaux is the en primeur system, which sees the latest vintage onto the market; for more on en primeur, see page 143.

The En Primeur System

En primeur is a method for purchasing wine in which the latest vintage is offered for sale before the wines have even been bottled. You pay for the wine often more than a year in advance of receiving it. Invitations to buy Bordeaux en primeur appear during the spring following the vintage, once the world's wine trade and press have visited the region for a week of tasting – usually the first week of April – in order to judge the quality.

The trick with buying en primeur is to engage with one or several merchants, establish the prices at which you will buy (and, for the expensive wines, the prices at which you won't). You won't usually be able to taste the wines yourself first (although some merchants run primeur tastings for a fee), so you will be reliant on the views of those who have. Thus you need arm yourself with some opinions. Try my website (www.thewinedoctor.com – I publish notes on all the wines I taste at the primeurs there) or track down the many other reports available online such as those from Jancis Robinson (www.jancisrobinson.com), Robert Parker and Neal Martin (both www.erobertparker.com). Most require a subscription or some sort of payment.

A Guide to Safe Buying En Primeur

Stick with trusted merchants you are familiar with, preferably those with a track record of selling en primeur, even if they're slightly more expensive. Certainly don't be tempted by 'cold-callers' making en primeur offers (usually with the promise of financial gain).

Stay current with news on wine fraud with expert Jim Budd's websites (investdrinks-blog.blogspot.co.uk and jimsloire.blogspot.com). Pay with a credit card, as this may offer protection if the wine never materialises. Know when to expect delivery. Using www.cellartracker.com (see page 136) is a good way of tracking your purchases.

BUYING EN PRIMEUR: THE PROS

- Secures stock of sometimes hard-to-find wines.
- Secures provenance – you know exactly where the wine has been.
- You can choose the bottling format – magnums, bottles or halves/splits.
- Buying early should secure the best price; historically this has been true, although this rule has broken down in recent vintages because of high release prices.

BUYING EN PRIMEUR: THE CONS

- Hard to get wines may be sold on allocation to established customers, or there may be a 'tie-in' requiring you to buy other wines as well.
- Sales are usually only of cases of six or twelve bottles, although some merchants will deal in smaller quantities.
- Sometimes small quantities are dripped onto the market; pushing prices up.

- En primeur is an interest-free unsecured loan; there is risk involved. See my guide to buying.
- The prices may exclude local taxes; if so, remember you will get hit with this bill when the wines are delivered.
- Release prices are higher than they used to be, and there is a chance they may fall after you have bought.

Professional Storage

've already provided some detail on how to cellar wine at home on page 135, but for those where this simply isn't an option there are plenty of companies out there who will store it for you. Of course, storage – not just of wine, but of all manner of things – is big business these days, and renting a self-storage unit is de rigueur for those in need of a little extra space. These aren't ideal for wine though; the conditions (especially the temperature) may not be perfect, the security might be somewhat less than adequate, and some such businesses prohibit the storage of foodstuffs (and they may consider wine to be in this category). Instead, turn to a dedicated wine storage company to look after your wine.

In times gone by it was quite common to store your wine with the merchant who had sold it to you. This was often inexpensive, and one benefit was that if you ultimately decided you would rather sell your wine than drink it, then it was in exactly the right place. Unfortunately there are problems with this approach. It's not unheard of for unscrupulous merchants to use your wine as if it were stock, selling it as required, replacing it at a later date; the wine which you thought had perfect provenance could in fact have been picked up from a dodgy auction for a song. And if the merchant declares bankruptcy, the wine will be viewed as an asset unless you can prove your ownership. Is the wine labelled as yours?

PROFESSIONAL STORAGE: DISADVANTAGES

- Wine can be inaccessible, and withdrawal might be whole cases only.
- Regular yearly storage fees mount up over time.

Much better is to seek out a dedicated business, one where the sole aim is to store, catalogue and generally nurture your wines until the time comes when you decide to drink them, or sell them. There will be a storage charge and this may vary according to how much you want to store, so pay attention to the small print. Some operations have huge underground caverns where the wine is handled only by employees and access by you and I is unlikely, whereas other units might offer individual lockers to which you can gain access. In some cases you can have wine delivered direct into storage, in others it's up to you to take your wine there. It all varies, so shop around, and find a solution that is right for you. A popular choice in the UK is Octavian (www.octavianvaults.co.uk); in the US most cities have storage options, like that at Seattle Wine Storage (www.seattlewinestorage.biz).

PROFESSIONAL STORAGE: ADVANTAGES

- Controlled, monitored environment perfect for wine.
- Insurance may be included (if not, it is essential you obtain some).
- Ensures provenance and thus value.
- 'Bonded' facilities may allow deferral of payment of taxes.

Bordeaux: Tracking Value

I t is clear that top Bordeaux – and many other wines of course – accrue in value over time. Sometimes that simply reflects the increased desirability of the wine as it matures, while reduced supply – as bottles are drunk – may also have some influence. Sometimes other factors may be important, such as demand from a new market, as we have seen with Asian demand for Château Lafite-Rothschild and its second wine Carruades de Lafite in recent years. For the former, gains are reasonably certain (especially if the wine has been highly rated by the critic with the biggest influence on Bordeaux pricing: Robert Parker) but tend to be long-term; prices often only really picking up after several years. In the case of the latter, prices based on new and sudden interest are perhaps more likely to fluctuate, and that which has rocketed skywards also has the potential to crash earthwards. The gains may be impressive, so might be the losses!

The question is, how to keep track of these changes in the Bordeaux marketplace, and how to keep tabs on the value of your cellar?

The first port of call may well be Cellar-Tracker! (www.cellartracker.com) again, as discussed on page 136. This excellent piece of software tracks the value of your cellar, using data from the CellarTracker! community or US-based auction websites. Alternatively, searching for current retail prices might provide some useful information, and this can easily be achieved using Wine Searcher (www.wine-searcher.com), with the advantage that this site also allows historical searches, so that you can see the value of your wine several months or even up to four years ago. Nevertheless, this becomes tedious when tracking the value of more than a couple of different wines, and something else is required.

Without doubt the next place to go for market and value data are the published auction and trading reports. The World of Fine Wine (www. finewinemag.com), perhaps the best wine magazine in print today, provides a useful quarterly report on wine auction activity, detailing all the successes – and failures – of the auction market in the UK, USA, Hong Kong and elsewhere around the globe. To see how the fine wine market is moving, though, the place to go is Liv-ex (www.liv-ex.com), the Fine Wine Exchange. Established in 1999, Liv-ex is a global internet and phone-based trading platform for wine, with members in 33 countries over six continents. If a wine is being traded, then the likelihood is that the trade will be through Liv-ex, who therefore have a very strong handle on market prices. These trades can be viewed live, but perhaps more informative are the fine wine indices which summarise the market, exactly as the FTSE 100 or Dow Jones indices do for stocks and shares. There are several indices, although the most commonly quoted are the Fine Wine 100 Index, which represents the price movement of 100 of the most sought-after wines on the strong secondary market, and the Fine Wine 50 Index, which tracks the movement of 50 wines from the first growths.

Investment Report

t is not just improved quality but also investment and speculation that has pushed the prices of the top cru classé Bordeaux – the most popular investment choice above all other wine regions – beyond the reach of most drinkers. Today there is a global trading platform dedicated to Bordeaux (www.liv-ex.com) and a thriving international trade. Across the world more nations are latching on to the delights of wine, China and India being notable new awakenings, so demand – and values – have continued to rise. No wonder there are now investment funds based purely on wine.

2011 report

The story of 2011 has been a mixed one as far as Bordeaux and the marketplace are concerned. The value of Bordeaux as summarised by the Liv-Ex Fine Wine 100 Index continued to climb until July. The big news came in the six months that followed, with a profound drop in the index to 14.85% below its January 2011 level. With a 3.9% drop in December 2011 alone there was no reassuring sign of an immediate slow up in this slide. Indeed, the fall in this latter index was the fourth largest since it was created in 2000. As an aside, auction sales also slowed during 2011, dropping from a 75% climb in value during 2010 to a 'mere' 14% in 2011. Having said that, the first few months of 2012 did see these indices regain some ground.

Nevertheless there has certainly been some correction in wine prices in the past year, albeit a small one when taken across the board. Although in some individual cases the

effect was not so small; Lafite-Rothschild 2008, for example, saw more than 40% wiped off its value. Of course the biggest climbers are always likely to be the biggest fallers, and Lafite 2008 is a case in point. Released at a relatively 'low' value it was soon trading at prices more than eight-times higher. Unusually for a wine (because fools like you or I might think the value was related to the quality of the wine, or influential point scores – not entirely true, I'm afraid) the value was greatly bolstered as recently as October 2010 by decoration of the bottle with a Chinese figure 8, further stoking up Asian demand. But if there's a wine destined for a tumble, surely it is one that sees rising price fluctuations based on labelling?

Look back a year, though, and we see that the 100 Index is still considerably above its January 2010 position, and continuing back in time it is also way above its value in January 2009, 2008 and 2007. And let us not forget how the index was fashioned back in January 2004; it kicked off with a value of 100, and so its value in December 2011 – 286.33 – means the portfolio of wines within the index are trading at 2.8 times their value seven years ago; investors with a long term plan are still very much in the winning.

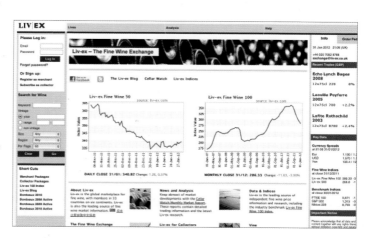